CONTENTS

CONTENTS

SHANGHAI
DAISY

The autobiography of Daisy Kwok

Edited and presented by Tess Johnston & Graham Earnshaw

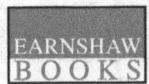

EARNSHAW
BOOKS

Shanghai Daisy

By Daisy Kwok

ISBN-13: 978-988-8552-39-9

This book has been reset in 10pt Book Antiqua. Spellings and punctuations are left as in the original edition.

Biography / Autobiography

EB113

Published by Earnshaw Books Ltd. (Hong Kong)

PREFACE

By Graham Earnshaw

DAISY KWOK's life spanned old Shanghai and modern Shanghai, old China and "New" China, in a way that no other did. She was born in 1908 in Australia into a Cantonese family that in 1918 made a big move to Shanghai, and became very rich. Her father built and owned the Wing On Department Store on Shanghai's main thoroughfare, Nanking Road, and for three decades, Daisy led the life of the rich and famous in one of the world's most dazzling cities. Then, after the Communist takeover in 1949, she spent three decades being denounced as a "capitalist." After that, thankfully, there was more than a decade of relative calm. She died in 1998 in Shanghai, which had by then been her home for eighty years.

This book presents reminiscences about her life, written by her in the early and mid-1990s. I met her in 1995, introduced by Tess Johnston, who has also provided a postscript to this book. Daisy showed me some of what she had written, having started while attending a writing class on a trip to see her siblings in the United States in 1987, and I encouraged her to write more with the intention of publishing it in some form, some day. She readily agreed, and I spent many afternoons with her discussing her stories. She was very interested that her memories be preserved for posterity. Twenty years later, it has come time to return to her writings, and Tess and I have edited them only lightly, to preserve Daisy's effervescence for the reader.

Let me first provide an overview of the time and the place. The story of Daisy cannot be separated from that of Shanghai, the city in which she spent most of her life, and the city and its history has the same rich mixture of influences and the same equivocal status as did Daisy. Chinese or international? It was hard to say categorically, and the best answer was both.

Here is a quick history and exposition of some of the key elements that made Shanghai so special. It began as a small fishing and trading town on the mudflats of the Huangpu River, in no way a significant place. British opium smugglers in the early nineteenth century had traded through and near it, and decided it would make a good base for expanded and regularized business activities after the first Opium War came to its inevitable conclusion in 1842, with the complete rout of the Manchu Empire's obsolescent and unprepared military in the face of advanced British technology. Europe, it turned out, had taken the idea of gunpowder and used it for something other than fireworks.

The British took Hong Kong Island in perpetuity as a colony, but Shanghai and a few other cities along the coast — the principal opium transshipment points — were opened to foreigners as concessions, not colonies. It was to become an important distinction in terms of the way the Chinese and foreigners interacted in Shanghai.

China in the later nineteenth century was a mess. The Manchu Empire of which it had been a part for over two hundred years was losing its grip, and the country was wracked by wars, lawlessness, famine and general social disruption. The Yangtze River delta region of which Shanghai is a part, has long been a land of deep prosperity thanks largely to fish and rice. The flat lands to the west of the foreigner-ruled city were filled with prosperous families, and waves of lawlessness pushed them to find a haven, and they found one in the international settlements of Shanghai where foreign law held sway. While it was for the benefit of the foreign traders that modern Shanghai was founded, it was the Chinese who most vigorously grasped the opportunity that it represented. They moved in, they built and pushed up land prices, established businesses and took full advantage of what international law created in this small enclave.

Among those who were attracted by the huge commercial potential of Shanghai, perched on the edge of China but not then under Chinese control, were the Kwoks from Australia. But there were many other groups as well. The large Cantonese community played an intermediary role between Real China and the foreigners, almost none of whom bothered to learn Chinese or take an interest in Chinese culture. These Cantonese people very often had English as their main language outside of the home, as Daisy did.

Then there were the Jews, of whom there were two distinct groups. The first to arrive, on the coattails of the British Empire as with the Cantonese, were the Sephardic Jews, originating from places like Damascus and Bombay. Some of the richest foreigners in old Shanghai, with family names such as Hardoon, Kadoorie and Sassoon, were Sephardic Jews. Victor Sassoon, the wealthiest and most successful property magnate in Shanghai prior to 1949, and also an avid horse racing fan, famously quipped: "There is only one race better than the Jews and that is the Derby."

Then in the 1920s and 1930s arrived another group, Ashkenazi Jews from Europe, mostly refugees and poorer. But they were also an important part of the rich and diverse mix that was Daisy's Shanghai.

During the early decades of the twentieth century, through World War I (1914–1918) and right though the Depression of the early 1930s, Shanghai's economy continued to boom and grow, until by 1937 it was the fifth largest city in the world and definitely one of the most prosperous. Then came the Japanese invasion in August of that year, an event that changed the fate of China, and certainly of Shanghai. The foreign concessions where Daisy and her family lived were not occupied by the Japanese until the end of 1941, but war changes everything, and the old Shanghai died in the midst of what became known to most of the world as the Pacific War.

Extraterritoriality, the convention under which foreigners in China were exempt from Chinese law, was abolished in 1943. In 1945, after the Japanese surrendered in the face of nuclear attacks by the Americans, the Nationalist Chinese government of Chiang Kai-shek resumed control of most of China. But the Communist guerrillas during the years of the Japanese war had morphed from an isolated band of guerrillas to becoming a serious political and military force, and the civil war that ensued pushed the Nationalists off the mainland to Taiwan. The Red Army marched into Shanghai on May 27, 1949, and the People's Republic of China was declared in Beijing by Chairman Mao on October 1.

This was the end of the world as Shanghai had known it, and the foreigner residents and many, if not most, of the wealthy Chinese, left the city, and also left China. Most of Daisy's siblings and relatives went to the United States, to Hong Kong, to Singapore anywhere but stay in Shanghai. But Daisy stayed, for reasons she explains in her narrative.

I spent a lot of time with Daisy in the mid-1990s, visiting her at her one-room home on Hunan Road in what had once been the western edge of the French Concession. She lived in an old mansion shared with a number of other families. I also occasionally had the honor of squiring her around the city. We

4

went to her huge former family home, a mansion of Swiss design now occupied by dozens of families, and to her former school, then and still today the top girls' school in Shanghai, where she was greeted by the school administrators, quite rightly, with great respect. We went to the so-called "Marshall House," a mansion in which General Marshall camped in the late 1940s as he tried to stem the fall of the Nationalist government, and she insisted on walking round the gardens and inspecting every flower and shrub along the way. We went to restaurants and nightspots in a chauffeured car — I was working for a foreign news agency at the time and had a company car and driver — and it was a wonderful thing to be able to give her a taste of the life she had once had, one more time. I saw her last on the day before she died, and she said words to me that in effect meant "goodbye," but it didn't hit me until afterwards.

This is not Daisy's full life story, it is episodic only. But it is still one of the richest and most valuable memoirs to come out of the dramatic arc of the history of 20th century Shanghai. There are stories from her life in Australia and youth in Shanghai, and many tales and references to her siblings. Daisy was one of nine children, who included Percy, the eldest, second brother Leon, eldest sister Pearlie, as well as Edie, George, Terry, Romie and Wally. There are indirect mentions of the arrest of her husband during the anti-Rightist campaign in 1957 and her own troubles during the Great Leap Forward in the late 1950s and in the Cultural Revolution of the late 1960s and beyond. I think she decided to not dwell in too much detail on these events because she was always forward-looking, always curious about new things, and never given to dwelling on the past. Regardless of her thinking and motives, she put up with it all. What shines through these pages is her positive spirit even in the midst of the most desperate of tragedies, such as the death of her husband in prison in 1961 after three years' incarceration stemming from his background — he also was deemed a "capitalist" — and the destruction of her photo albums by the Red Guards in the late 1960s.

Daisy in her 1980s was physically very petite, although there was still signs of the figure she refers to in her writings. Her hair was shocking white, and she laughed at people who asked if she had dyed it, pointing out practically that there is only one color that cannot be achieved in hair dyeing, which is natural white. But the most prominent aspect of her physically, apart from her shining eyes, were her hands. They were shriveled into little arthritically cramped claws, her fingers weak and deformed due to years of forced labor in freezing conditions during the Cultural Revolution. She never complained about it, and said they didn't hurt her, but just looking at her hands told a very sad story.

Daisy's main language was English. In high school and even at university in Peking, where she studied for four years, all tuition was in English, and most of her friends, while Chinese, were also perfectly comfortable with English. She spoke pretty good Cantonese, pretty good Shanghainese and pretty good Mandarin, too, by the time I met her. But in 1949, she could hardly read Chinese, and she was very proud of having learned to read the language — the simplified characters of today's China — as part of her reconstruction from "capitalist" to proletarian retiree. English, however, was her first language.

Sudden changes in life circumstances are very destabilizing, but going from very poor to very rich is much easier than the alternative. What is most amazing about Daisy is that she fell from the very pinnacle of Shanghai society to the very depths and her positive character made it possible for her to accept and face everything that came along. She firmly refused to ever have any regrets. She told me of acquaintances who had handled the changes less well, sometimes by stepping out of windows in tall buildings.

The changes to life in Shanghai didn't take place immediately after the communists arrived in 1949. It was a more gradual process, and there is a book yet to be written about Shanghai post-1949. Life continued remarkably unchanged for many years for many people in many ways, through to the end of the 1950s. Daisy refers to the "Park Hotel's new restaurant in the penthouse" somewhere in the mid-1950s, and if the Park was still opening a new restaurant at that point, people other than the lumpen proletariat were around to dine there. Daisy still had a maid in 1966, although that situation didn't end well, as you will see.

There are a few other stories that she told me that do not appear in these pages. Once when she was convalescing in hospital in the early 1930s, she was visited by Madame Soong May-ling, the wife of the supreme leader, Generalissimo Chiang Kai-shek, reflecting the close ties between the Cantonese diaspora of which Daisy and her father was a part and the ruling elite of the Republic of China. One year, she was chosen at a beauty pageant as "Miss Shanghai". She was invited to a dinner at the Cathay Hotel hosted by its owner, the property magnate Sir Victor Sassoon, who seated her next to him at the dining table and on several occasions placed his hand on her thigh. Each time, she gently pushed it off.

In her writings, she mentions Albert Suez, to whom she first became engaged. In the end she cut off the engagement, which left Albert distraught in a way that is worth reading: I won't give the game away here. But Albert's full name was Kyeu Yong Albert Suez, and he was the son of Dr I. C. Suez, a prominent

Shanghai doctor. He ended up marrying Rhoda How in a society wedding in Shanghai on October 29, 1932. Daisy, meanwhile, married Y.H., by whom she had two children. After his death, she married again, but it lasted only for two years before he too died, of cancer.

It has been an emotional experience reading and helping to edit this manuscript because I knew Daisy so well. She was modest about how she had handled the trials of her life, but she was still quietly proud of having survived it all, and of not leaving China, as everyone else in the Kwok family did. She met all the trials in her life with poise, wisdom and quick-witted resolution, and ultimately faced down her persecutors. She would never have said this herself, but it is true: she was better then they were.

EDITING NOTES

We have not changed the timing of her references. Most of the spelling throughout is English rather than American, reflective of her early upbringing in Australia and the predominance of British English in old Shanghai. We have basically left it as she wrote it.

INTRODUCTION

By Daisy Kwok

I STARTED WRITING this some time before I left for my trip to visit my son in America in December 1987. I started by making a draft in an exercise book and when I got to Arizona, I tried to put it into shape and began typing it out. So many people, mainly my son Deedums, have told me to write, so I did a few pages while staying with his family.

I'm sorry to say that those few pages are as far as I got. Since this month of September, I have been more or less laid up with a bad leg. I really don't know whether it was due to a fall I had or whether it is arthritis. Anyway, I can't walk properly, so I can't go out. I've been feeling very sorry for myself and haven't done anything except complain. Today I realized that this attitude is getting me nowhere, so I have decided not to waste any more time and I shall start making another copy of what I have written so far, and add some more if I possibly can.

Elsie had written me about Leon's writing an account of our Kwok Family background. She mentioned that she intended correcting some of the statements in it. It wasn't until both Elsie and Leon had passed away that I finally got a copy of Leon's article from Georgie. As soon as I read it I felt that I also wanted to record some reminiscences of my early life. My biggest regret is that Leon's article did not reach me until after Pearlie had passed away, as I would have liked to have consulted with her son on many points. I also regret that Pearlie did not read Leon's

INTRODUCTION

article as I know she would have enjoyed it very much. Time is passing rapidly and I wonder if I'll be able to put down all I want to record.

While I was staying with Edie in New York, Helen Tsang came to see me. I last saw her in Shanghai before Liberation so we had a lot to talk about. She also gave me a whole lot of photocopies of newspaper clippings about the Dress Salon "Tsingyi" which we had founded in the Park Hotel in Shanghai in 1936. I had lost all my photos during the Cultural Revolution [1966–1976]. I didn't have a chance to go over them thoroughly until I returned to Shanghai. There, they resulted in another flood of memories.

On that trip to the States and Singapore from December 1987 to June 1988, I was lucky also to receive copies of photos that I had lost during the Cultural Revolution. Looking at them brought back memories of incidents I had almost forgotten. So now I find myself just writing at random, jotting anything that comes into my mind as I look at some of those pictures.

Now where shall I begin?

AUSTRALIA

I KNOW VERY little about my grandparents, paternal or maternal, but I do remember hearing that grandfather Ma (Mum's father) was a Christian minister. Our whole family thought so. But while at Romie's place during Christmas in 1987, he showed me a letter from Terry, in which he mentioned that according to Mum's birth certificate, a copy of which he had managed to get while on a trip to Australia earlier in the year, it seems that Mum's father was a fruit merchant from Macau.

Perhaps this is the reason for the confusion. Mum was born in Bourke, and when she went to Sydney, she stayed with a minister's family by the name of Young Way. It was there that she met our father. Her close association with the Young Way family probably made us think her father was a minister, whereas he was actually her guardian.

There were five children in the Ma family, four daughters and a son; Mum was the eldest. Her only brother, Ma Seng Young, also came to Shanghai, where Dadda gave him a job with his Wing On Company. (My sister Pearlie and I later visited the family when they lived in one of the Wing On Terrace houses just after he passed away.)

Mum's name was Darling, named after the Darling River, one of the longest in Australia. When I was very young and I heard Dadda calling her by her name, I wondered how he could he use such endearing terms in public! I did not know then that it was actually her name. Mum married Dadda when she was only 16 years old.

My father's name was George and his Chinese name was Kwok Bew. According to Chinese custom the surname is given first, but he was generally known as George Bew. In fact, we all used the surname Bew while in Australia.

I was born in Campbell Street, Sydney, on April 2, 1909, as the seventh child. Later on, we moved to Dowling Street in a house opposite a public park. All I remember of the house is that I had diphtheria there and passed it on to Edie and Percy and was kept isolated on the porch. When I was about four or five, we moved to No. 2 Croydon Street in Petersham, where Dadda had bought a house. There were two gardens, a large chicken coop, a pigeon loft, stables for our two ponies, and a yard with a well in it, although no longer in use. (I have given a detailed description of the house below.)

I started with kindergarten, and then attended the primary school on Crystal Street just around the corner from where we lived. On Sundays we went to Sunday School at the Cantonese Church downtown that our parents attended. Dadda gave Elsie, Wally and me each a penny for the collection box. One day on our way to Sunday School, Wally said he would show us another route. He stopped at an ice-cream parlor and suggested we have an ice-cream cone. He told me to use the penny to buy the cone and use the half-penny change for the collection plate. That was Wally! However, I always did what he told me to do.

There was much racial discrimination in both schools. The children at Sunday School called me all sorts of names, so I decided not to go there again. One day, the headmaster came to find out what was wrong. My mother answered the doorbell. I followed her to the door and when I saw who it was, I hid behind her. When I heard his complaint, I stepped forward and told him I was not going to attend Sunday School as long as I was being called names.

Every Saturday night, Dadda killed two chickens for our Sunday lunch. Wally had a rooster that he had tamed and it would strut around proudly as though claiming to be ruler of the roost. Memories of our Sunday lunches stand out vividly. Mum and Dadda, dressed in their Sunday best, Dad in his frock coat and top hat, attended the Cantonese Presbyterian Church. After church, he brought home some of his friends for lunch and this meal was always a sumptuous one. Our maid did the cooking and at times extra help was even called in.

Dad did not have much education but he had the ability to adapt. I remember him taking Mum and Edie to the Opera or to see a new play. I loved watching Mum and Edie dressing up for these occasions and there was always a box of chocolates included. How I wished I could hurry and grow up so that I could be included in these outings!

Leon recorded Dad's experience with his new Harley-Davidson motorbike, and I was there when the incident happened. Every Sunday morning, Dad would take us for a spin on the motorbike that had a sidecar. Mum sat in the sidecar with Georgie on her lap, I sat on a small seat in front of them and Elsie rode behind Dadda. I can still picture Dadda sprawled out on the road as the motorbike took off by itself, then he jumped up and chased it!

I have no recollection of an automobile that Leon has described, but I do remember our two ponies, Dolly and Nigger. We had a sulky (with two wheels) and a phaeton (with four) and how I admired Edie as she drove the sulky alone (as only one horse was needed for it). Dolly and Nigger were used to pull the phaeton when more members of the family went out together. When we were leaving for China, we had to sell the ponies. It almost broke my heart to see them one day drawing a heavy cart on the road. I called them by name and they seemed to recognize me.

It used to be Leon's job to take care of the ponies, but when he left for China with Percy and Pearlie in 1915, the task was taken over by Wally. He wasn't as conscientious as Leon and often tried to bribe me to feed them. Once he promised to give me a penny if I did so. After climbing up to the loft to get and mix the feed, I fed the ponies and I then asked for my penny. He told me to put out my hand. He put the penny in it – and then immediately took it back again. He said, "I promised to give you a penny, but I did not say you could keep it!" Again, that was Wally.

When I was told that the family was going to Shanghai, I did not understand what it really meant. At school I told my schoolmates that I was going to have a Chinese meal at the Shanghai Restaurant. That is what "Shanghai" meant to me.

When we later came up from Australia I was wearing Western-style clothes. I remember being so surprised to see Pearlie in a blue silk jacket and pants when she met our ship upon our arrival in Hong Kong. But by the time I graduated from high school, my wardrobe was entirely Chinese. When very young, it was Edie who decided what Elsie and I were to wear, but after she married, then Pearlie decided to take over. Originally my dresses were always made from imported material, in summer soft voiles or muslins. But Pearlie decided to use Chinese silks. She had the tailor make me a dress of blue silk with a Chinese design on it. In my eyes, it was not the material young girls should wear. I shuddered every time she insisted I wear that dress. Then once she had a hat made for me of white *crepe de chine*. It had a wide floppy brim with a scarf that hung over one side. I hated it, but Pearlie forced me to wear it. (I thought of this when I saw a photograph taken in the garden of our Croydon Street house – and in it Pearlie, Elsie and I are all wearing velvet dresses.) My solution to this problem was to decide to start wearing Chinese style clothing.

I was in the kindergarten class of the Crystal Street public school in Sydney. There were about thirty pupils in the class and our seats were arranged in a circle in the classroom. One morning, the teacher showed us a bottle of milk.

"We are going to make butter," she said.

We watched eagerly as she passed the bottle to the first pupil.

"Shake it vigorously for a minute or so, and then pass it to the one sitting beside you."

Each pupil was to shake the bottle as it came into her hand and then pass it on. Soon we began to notice little dots of butter clinging to the sides of the bottle.

"Keep on shaking," the teacher told us.

Then the bell rang. It was time for morning recess.

"Those who wish to go out and play, may do so, but those who wish to keep on making butter may remain here. Do whichever you prefer."

Two of my little friends came over to me and whispered, "Let's go out and finish that game of hopscotch we started yesterday."

It isn't easy to make friends when one is the only Chinese in the class so I was grateful for their friendliness and immediately agreed, and off we went. We returned to the classroom when the bell rang again. We were surprised to find our chairs were placed outside the circle, and we were told to sit there.

The shaking by those in the circle continued, and they smiled expectantly as the lump of butter grew bigger until the teacher announced that it was done. She gave each pupil a slice of bread and then spread it with the newly-made butter. We got none.

"This is to punish you for wanting to go off and play instead of wanting to learn to make butter," the teacher explained.

To me it was no explanation at all. After all, she had offered us a choice. Were we to be punished because we chose to go out?

THE HOUSE WE LIVED IN

No. 2 Croydon Street, Petersham, Sydney

RECENTLY I HAD a letter from my brother Georgie in Honolulu telling me he had a picture of our old family homestead in Australia. He had just taken a trip to Sydney and had visited the old house, which was still there. The news brought back so many memories that I asked him to send it to us. I was eight years old when we left Australia, but I still had a vivid memory of the house.

The main entrance had a gate which led to the steps before the front door. However, I usually entered by turning to the right and going into the garden and then around to a back entrance. There were two gardens, the first was what we called the Rose Garden. Dadda loved flowers, especially roses, so the flower beds were full of different varieties. At the end of this garden was a trellis which was covered with a climbing variety of roses. Beyond the trellis was the second garden, with a lawn in the middle and flower beds surrounding it. There was a pigeon house at the end of the garden.

Beside this garden was what we called the "well yard" as there was a well, but of course no longer with any water in it. From this yard I could enter the house by steps which led to an enclosed porch. Beyond the well yard were the stables for our two ponies. A gate in this yard was the back entrance through which the sulky and phaeton could go.

It was an old fashioned two-storeyed house. When we moved

in, the gas jets were still there but we used electricity. The front door opened into a long hallway. On the left was the living room or parlor, a very large room. I remember that it was big enough to hold two sets of furniture. On the other side of the hall were two rooms. The first was called the study, but actually in it was a long table on which Dad kept albums of photos of his old cronies. When they came to visit, they would go over them to recall their earlier days together. We youngsters were not very interested in these albums, but to Dadda they were his prize possessions and he even took them back to China with us.

These three rooms were not often used except for entertaining, and especially for the Sunday lunches which I described elsewhere. Breakfast and lunch were eaten in the kitchen but dinner was served in the dining room. (As a rule, we ate Western-style food, as our maid was an Australian.) Next to the kitchen was the laundry. A side entrance in the kitchen opened onto a lane which led to Croydon Street. That completed the ground floor.

A broad stairway at the end of the hall led to two hallways, one lower than the other. The larger one on the right led towards the front of the house where there were five bedrooms. The first two overlooked the street from a long veranda and were my father's and mother's rooms. Next to Dadda's room on the right of the hall was Leon and Wally's room. Opposite them were two smaller rooms, one for Edie and the other for Pearlie and Elsie. I slept in Dadda's room and Georgie in Mum's. The other hallway led past two rooms to the bathroom and the toilet. Percy occupied the first room while the other was for the maid. That is the house as I remember it.

Incidentally, what happened to Dad's treasured albums was not pleasant. After he had unpacked them when we settled down in the Tsongchow Road house in Shanghai, Dad once more laid them out on a long table in the room next to the dining room. When Pearl came to Shanghai after finishing her studies in Hong Kong, she took over the housekeeping. She decided the space was wasted on those old albums, so she put them away in a cupboard. After a while she thought they still occupied too much room so she threw them away without even asking Dadda's permission. It so happened that one day Dadda brought home an old friend from Australia. He wanted to show him pictures of their old pals. When he couldn't find the albums he asked Pearl for them. She told him she had gotten rid of them. Dad was nearly heartbroken, but all he said was, "Pearlie, how could you?"

ADOLESCENCE

IN 1917, we left Sydney on a Japanese steamer, the *Tango Maru* and arrived in Hong Kong about six weeks later. On the ship I stuck with Wally as much as I could and I suppose I got on his nerves.

One day he said "Okay, we'll play "Follow the Leader" and see if you are smart enough to follow me."

I followed him around and finally he walked into the Men's Lavatory. That did not stop me and I went in too. He had to get me out fast before anyone found me there!

While in Hong Kong we stayed in a hotel and there always seemed to be a strange odor in the air. When we got to Shanghai and stayed in another hotel I found the same odor. It wasn't until many years later that I learned it was the smell of opium.

While in Hong Kong, Dad sent for his Kwok relatives to come from our native village, then called Heng Shan but now known as Chungshan. They were complete strangers to me. Not being able to speak a word of Chinese, we could only stare at each other. I remember their pulling up my skirt to see what I was wearing underneath. Of course, for our parents it was a very happy reunion. It seemed that there were more Ma relatives in Hong Kong than Kwoks. Most of them spoke English, as they had also come from Australia.

Arriving in Shanghai in early 1918, we stayed at the Tung Ya Hotel which was part of the Sincere Company that was opened by the Ma family. My father had come to open the Shanghai

Wing On Company, owned by the Kwoks. The hotel was directly opposite the site where the Wing On was being built. It fascinated me to see the five-storey building being built. It was surrounded by bamboo scaffolding and one day during a violent storm the scaffold blew down, causing such a commotion!

While living in the hotel, my mother caught smallpox. We weren't allowed to see her but still at times I managed to steal into her room; I bet the others did too. One day as I gazed out of the window I saw white things floating around in the air. I opened the window and collected some in my hand. I rushed to my mother's room to ask her what they were, but when I opened my hand there was nothing there but water. Mum laughed and explained that it was snow. It had never snowed in Sydney.

Our uncle Gocklock, whose first wife was my mother's sister, also lived in the hotel. He was to be managing director of the new Wing On Company with my father. He had a Ford car, which was considered a luxury in those days. Sometimes he took us out for a drive to the countryside. Actually we only went as far as the Bubbling Well, but at that time it was all just open space. We felt we had driven a long, long way.

After a few months we rented a house on Tsongchow Road. These terrace houses were mainly occupied by members of the British Police Force. Not being able to speak Chinese, I found it easy to mix with the British children of my own age who lived there.

Next we had to find schools. Being Cantonese, my father put us in a Cantonese school. Elsie, Wally and I were sent to the Sun Kwong Cantonese School in the Hongkew district, far away from where we lived. I believe my two eldest brothers studied elsewhere. Pearlie had been left in Hong Kong to finish her schooling at St. Stephen's Girls' College.

Every morning we all piled into the family's Buick to be taken to our various destinations. Dad to the W.O. office, Leon to his office on Kiangse Road, and I am not sure but by then I think Percy had already gone to the United States to study. The three of us were dropped off at our school and then Mum went to the Hongkew market, which she went to without fail every morning.

In the afternoon the car came to pick us up, all except for Dad (Mum had already gone home after marketing). Dadda stayed to work – or rather to enjoy the W.O. Roof Garden which was an amusement centre offering different types of entertainment: movies, acrobatic shows, Peking or Cantonese opera, etc. Dad never returned home until late at night after the roof garden had closed.

The first thing the teacher at the school decided was to give us Chinese names. He tried to make them sound as near as possible to our English names, thus Elsie was called "An Ci", meaning Peace and Kindness, Wally was "Hui De", Wisdom and morality/virtue. And I? I never found out what name I was given. The names were written on small slips of paper to show our father for his approval. I proudly clutched my paper in my hand, but as luck would have it, as I got into the car a gust of wind blew it away. I didn't know what to do. I told Percy my plight and he asked me if I remembered the sound of the words. I didn't. Then he wrote down the two words "Ding Shi" and asked if those were the characters. In my ignorance all characters looked alike, so from then on I was known by the queer name of "Ding Shi" which meant "certain time."

It wasn't until I was ready to graduate from McTyeire High School in 1928 that I realised the name was not very appropriate. All through my school days I was known as "Daisy" and I didn't like the idea of that queer Chinese name appearing on my graduation diploma. A classmate of mine, Mang Yuin Kya, gave me a new name. She admired the writer Bing Xin and named me after her. So on my graduation diploma, my new name appeared for the first time. In college I was known as Guo Wan Ying.

Life at the Cantonese school was a nightmare for me. All three of us, in spite of the difference in ages, were put in the first grade to begin learning Chinese. I just could not pronounce the words correctly. Every day I just cried and cried. Then we were put in the highest class for our English lessons. Elsie and Wally had no difficulty there – after all, they were three and five years older than I. Again, I ran into difficulties and I couldn't keep up. The reader was too difficult for me.

Lunch time was another problem as we had to find a restaurant to have this meal. We found one on Szechuan Road near the bridge that crosses the Soochow Creek. We went there by rickshaw, Elsie and Wally on the seat while I sat on Wally's lap. He always complained that my bones stuck into him and it wasn't very comfortable for me either. One day he suggested that we walk back to school instead of taking the rickshaw that cost seven cents. He said we could use the money to buy melon seeds and they would be divided into equal shares. Wally always gave himself the extra seed if there was one, as he explained it was his idea.

When we first went to the restaurant, we did not know how to order food as we did not speak Chinese and the waiters knew no English. Seeing some other customers eating noodles, we pointed and asked for the same. We learned this was called "*mien*" and every day we had *mien* for lunch.

Eventually a friend of our father, called Chen Bing Him, heard about us and insisted that we go to his home every day for lunch. The Chen family owned a big house on Range Road. My next problem was how to use chopsticks. No matter how hard I tried, I dropped food all over the table. I was so embarrassed and ashamed that I dreaded going there for this meal. The family noticed the predicament I was in and provided me with a spoon and fork. Many years later, I went to visit the family again. Out came the spoon and fork, but I pushed them aside and proudly showed them how expertly I could now handle chopsticks.

The Burlington Hotel was near the house we lived in. My elder sisters got to know some Chinese girls from Jamaica who had come to visit China. They knew about the McTyeire School and suggested that Elsie and I be sent there to study. It was a school run by American missionaries. (I think Wally was sent to the St. John's Middle School.) At McTyeire we had no language difficulty as all courses with the exception of Chinese were given in English. Actually, neglecting our study of Chinese was a big mistake, one I have regretted all my life. I did not realize how much I was handicapped until I graduated from college. However, at that time Shanghai was a city ruled by the "foreign imperialists" and everyone spoke English. It seemed more important to know English than Chinese. I remember attending a meeting of the Shanghai Chinese Women's Club and was surprised to find the meeting was conducted in English. Other international women's clubs held meetings in their own languages. In the big department stores, attendants had to know English to get a job. Even some rickshaw coolies could speak a few words.

When I was about to graduate from high school I had asked my father if I could go to college in America, as many of the McTyeire graduates did. He had just returned from a business trip to the States, and he did not approve of the way the youth studied there. He was definitely against my going abroad to study. So I wrote and asked him if he had any objections to my going to college in Peking. He gave his consent.

Actually I hadn't even intended to go to college; in those days not many girls went to college. I had just asked to go because some of my friends were there.

In order to be accepted, I needed a coach, they told me, because I would have to take an entrance test in trigonometry. I didn't even know what trig was, but I got a coach, a Yenching University student, and he said all you can do is just memorize all those facts. I did and I made the highest grade on the entry test.

During my freshman year I broke off my engagement to Albert Suez, Youth is not considerate and I realize now how much I must have hurt him, as well as his parents with whom I had stayed for almost a year. I do not blame them if they thought badly of me.

I went to Yenching University in 1929, majoring in Psychology, but it was not the psychology I had meant to study. My education was done all wrong, I studied the wrong thing. I had really wanted to study Psychoanalysis and wanted to do Psychiatry, but instead of that I wound up just experimenting with rats. So I spent the next four years there. I went home to visit the family during summer vacations, and sometimes in the winter holidays as well.

I never spoke the Peking dialect because I mixed with the Overseas Chinese, most of them from Honolulu. I graduated in 1933 and wanted to go to America to study interior decoration but my father said I couldn't go. He said the youth there "don't study, they just play, and they're wild – so you can't go."

SHANGHAI HOMES

WHEN RETURNING to China in 1918, we had brought back with us an old bicycle which used to belong to Leon. Wally claimed it as his, but he seldom rode it. It was an outdated model and was left in the hall beside the staircase in our Tsongchow Road house. I used to get on it and try to ride. When I lost my balance, I would lean against the wall or staircase. One day Wally found me on the bike. He looked at me condescendingly and said, "You don't know how to ride a bike." I claimed I did.

"All right," he said. "We'll take the bike outside and if you prove you can ride, I'll give it to you."

I didn't even know how to get on and start riding but I told him to give me a push after I had climbed on. He did, I rode round and round the block, but I couldn't stop because I did not know how to get off.

"All right,' he said, "you can have the bike."

I kept on riding until I was so exhausted that I fell off. Anyway, the bike was now mine! I used to ride to visit the Yung family who lived on Seymour Road, just around the corner from our place. Then I would ride to the Olympic Theatre near Carter Road (now called the Roxy Theatre) to take in a movie and in those days they had continuous shows. I had loads of fun with that old bike.

The Tsongchow Road house was rented and it did not have modern sanitary conveniences – not many houses did – but it had two bathrooms. Dad had visited many of his friends' homes that they had built and decided that he would also have a house built. The house was on Avenue Foch, opposite Hart Road. According to Chinese custom, it was large enough to house his sons and their families as well. At that time only Leon was married, but he and Dora wanted a place of their own and moved with their two young sons to a terrace house nearby. Unfortunately, the two babies died from meningitis and Leon and Dora then came to live with us at 771 Avenue Foch. (Edie was already married before the house was built.)

We had not lived there very long when Dad sold the house because he found the masons had forgotten to put down waterproofing material under the roof and when we had our first storm it rained inside as well as outside. Dad had the roof re-done and then sold the house.

Our next house was 19 Lucerne Road, a house built by a Swiss named Luthy. Dad was attracted by its beautiful garden and lawn.

The house still stands today, although the garden and lawn are now occupied by workers' flats. Our old house is now occupied by thirty-seven families and each room houses one family. The younger generation of Kwoks, however, always want to visit the old family homestead whenever they visit Shanghai.

Not long ago, the BBC asked me to take part in a documentary TV film they were making on "Famous Cities of the World." They wanted to know about life in Shanghai before "liberation" in 1949 and when I told them the old family house was still there, they asked me to take them to see it. I don't know the results of that film as they never sent me the video as they had promised.

During the Cultural Revolution all my photo albums were destroyed, more than 30 of them, but Edie sent me a picture of the family taken in front of the house during the 1920s. All of the family members are there, four brothers and four sisters, our parents, and the spouses and children of the married family members.

One evening many years later, I watched an episode of The Cosby Show on TV. I enjoyed it very much as one of the incidents was very similar to something I had experienced when I was young. In the show the adolescent daughter was rather upset because she lacked something her schoolmates had. She was so worried that she was afraid to attend school the next day. She thought her school mates would consider her odd. Her father and mother finally succeeded in getting her to confide in them. She was worried because she had not developed a bosom as the other girls her age had and she couldn't stand being different. Her parents succeeded in comforting her by explaining that she would develop normally when the right time came. Well, my problem was just the opposite – I thought I was *too* well developed for my age.

My sister-in-law Dora's mother was a wonderful knitter. They said that she would enter the cinema with a ball of wool and four needles and when the film was over, she came out with a pair of socks. She had knitted lovely dresses for her two youngest daughters. I thought they were so pretty that I couldn't help feeling envious. Dora knew how much I admired her mother's handiwork so she knitted me a beautiful rose-colored dress. How happy I was, and I couldn't wait to put it on. The dress seemed to fit perfectly and then I noticed it clung to my body and showed my protruding breasts. Each time I wore the dress, which wasn't often, I tried to hold my breath so that perhaps my breasts would not be so noticeable.

I often recalled this, but never told anyone about it. It is almost fifty years since I last saw Dora. She now lives in Manila taking care of an invalid daughter who had a stroke more than ten years ago and is paralyzed from the neck down, cannot talk or chew. Dora took her daughter to Manila after her husband, my brother Leon, died because it is so much cheaper to live there. Her daughter needs round-the-clock nursing and the amount they paid one nurse in the United States is enough to cover the salaries of three nurses in Manila who work in eight-hour shifts.

The Cosby Show reminded me of the rose-colored dress, and I thought of Dora and what a lonely life she must be leading since she left New York. Her other children live there and take turns visiting her and their bed-ridden sister, but that is not too often. I think Dora was happier when she was together with family and friends in New York. Our family members are growing fewer as the years go by, and now those who remain are all in their "twilight years." I decided to write to Dora to let her know I still thought of her. Part of my letter was as follows:

As one grows older it seems that memories of our younger days are much clearer than of more recent events. Hence I started writing my so-called memoir. There is one incident that I'd like to tell you about, or rather to explain. Do you remember during the early years of your marriage to Leon your mother had knitted dresses for your sisters, Mamie and Lulu? You knew I admired those dresses and you were good enough to make one for me. It was a lovely rose-colored dress and a perfect fit. I'm afraid at the time I did not show my appreciation and I do not blame you if you thought I was an ungrateful wretch. Once you asked me why I did not wear it – was it because I did not like it? I failed to answer.

Here is the reason I did not feel like wearing it. I really loved the dress and was so happy to put it on, but I noticed it showed my breasts which were developing at that time. In secret I would put the dress on to admire it, but when I noticed my protruding bosom I felt too ashamed to wear it outside. After a while you asked me to give it back, and I believe you ripped it up and made some sweaters for your young children.

When I recall this incident I regret so much that I did not have the sense then to explain to you why I did not wear the dress. But youth is not considerate and I was not thinking of how I might be hurting you, as I was more concerned about my own shape; in those days women were supposed to be flat-chested. How silly I was – I could have asked you to teach me how to wear a tight brassiere.

So that concludes this anecdote and almost seventy years later I am asking you to forgive me.

ENGAGEMENT

I GRADUATED from McTyeire School in 1928 and immediately came down with a severe case of typhoid fever. I was in the Country Hospital for seven weeks. At that time I was engaged to Albert Suez, who had left for the States to further his education after graduating from St. John's University in Shanghai. When my prospective father-in-law came back from the Foreign Service, he said I had to recuperate in Peking. I thought that was a good idea so I went to Peking with him. When I got to Peking I met a childhood friend, Suzanne Lu. Her father was at one time the Chinese consul in Australia and the Lu family had stayed with us when they first arrived there. I was five or six years old then and now our friendship was renewed. Suzanne was studying at Yenching University and introduced me to many of her college mates. They finally convinced me that I should go to college there instead of getting married.

When my fiancé came back from studying engineering in America, I told him I just didn't want to get married. He came to Yenching University to look for me and I hid in the Women's Library, and I looked out the window and saw him pacing up and down. Every summer I went to Tientsin and then on back to Shanghai. And there he was, waiting at the railway station for me. He had followed me, and he also had a home there.

"Look I've got a gun in my pocket and if you don't marry me I'm going to shoot you," he said.

"Good, shoot me," I replied. "And you still can't marry me."

He didn't shoot me. Then he went to my brothers and told them, "Make her marry me." They said, "How can we make her marry you? It's up to her to decide."

I gave him back the ring, a huge square diamond, and that was the end of that.

Meanwhile I had another boyfriend, one of my former professors. He later wanted me to go on for graduate work in France. Then when I got back to Shanghai, I met another man and he became my last boyfriend because I ended up marrying that one, and he became the father of my two children. He had studied in America and was a graduate of MIT, but unfortunately he had no head for business and he loved to gamble.

From the day we were engaged until the wedding day, six months later, I was kept busy planning everything for our new home. There was furniture to be bought or ordered, along with drapes, bed linen, carpets, kitchen appliances, chinaware, and I had to find and engage reliable servants. The guest list had to be made and the invitations sent out, then there was my clothing and, most important of all, my wedding gown. It was no wonder I lost weight and weighed only eighty-eight pounds by the time I thought I had done everything.

The night before the wedding I suddenly wondered what we should have for breakfast the next day. I had no idea what my husband-to-be (I called him Y.H.) was in the habit of eating. We had had lunches, teas, dinners and suppers together, but never a breakfast and, as far as I could recall, we had never even discussed such things. "Well, I'll have to plan something," I thought, "I can't let him find me an incompetent housewife."

My brain was twirling around. Should I serve a Chinese breakfast of *congee* (rice porridge) with its accompanying dishes of shredded meat, pickled cucumbers, peanuts, black eggs, beancurd, etc? Or would he prefer a foreign-style meal? Then

ENGAGEMENT

I remembered the Continental or English breakfasts I had been served in hotels where I had stayed in Manila and Hong Kong. I thought I couldn't go wrong if I did something like that.

I got up early the next morning to give my cook instructions on what to prepare for the first meal in our new home. When it was ready, I laid the table myself and then called my husband, announcing that breakfast was ready.

When we were seated at the table, the breakfast started off with fresh orange juice, then porridge with milk and sugar, next bacon and eggs with toast, butter and marmalade, finally ending with coffee with thick cream and sugar. I hardly ate anything as I was so busy serving him. At the end of the meal, I looked at him anxiously.

"Did you like it?" I asked. "Tell me, what do you usually have for breakfast?"

"Oh, this was fine," he said. "But actually I only have a glass of milk with a raw egg beaten in it for breakfast. What are you in the habit of eating?"

"Oh," I replied, "I only drink a cup of coffee."

What a relief it was to know I wouldn't have to go through the ordeal of preparing such a breakfast again.

MARRIED LIFE

I MARRIED Y.H. Woo in 1934. Our daughter Laurel, nicknamed Lollipop, was born in 1938 and our son, Leonard (always known as Deedums) was born in 1943. Y.H. was never good at making money and he was too fond of gambling. We hardly made ends meet but somehow I was able to put on a good show. At one time, I worked with the Chinese Medical Association, getting advertisements for their publications. The doctors working there did not like the idea of my paycheck being higher than theirs. I worked on a commission basis and they did not realize that I made more because I managed to get more ads for their magazines. But after 1941 when the Japanese came to Shanghai and took over many of the foreign firms, I did choose not to work for them.

I was friendly with Bernadine Fritz and worked closely with her at the International Arts Theatre. We did all sorts of programs, and since I was always interested in dramatics I did several plays with them. These were Chinese plays translated into English. I had an instructor to teach me all the techniques, etc., and it was fun. We even did puppet shows and made our own puppets. But this also ended when the Japanese came in and most of the foreigners had left Shanghai.

As I mentioned earlier, I started a dress salon with Helen Tsang and our studio was in the Park Hotel, near the race course. We used only Chinese materials and Helen designed the gowns while I managed the firm. That also came to an end when Helen's family left Shanghai in 1937. Because of the Japanese invasion, I was sent to Hong Kong with Mum, Pearlie and her two children, and I was then pregnant with Lollie. I did not like Hong Kong and returned to Shanghai in the midst of the fighting and gave birth to Lollie in Shanghai on January 2, 1938. There I was the only patient in Dr. Sun's maternity home. My son Deedums was later born there in 1943.

After victory over the Japanese, Y.H.'s cousin, S.Y. Liu, then the Minister of Finance, gave Y.H. a job with the organization that took over enemy property. Y.H. was put in the German property division and had an office in the old German firm, DEFAG. He became friendly with some Germans who used to work at the Schmidt Co., and together they started the firm Transmarina Scientific Supplies that imported scientific instruments from Germany.

CHRISTMAS CELEBRATIONS

WHILE TALKING TO Edie in New York when I stayed with her, I happened to mention our celebrating Christmas and birthdays in the old days. I was surprised when she said she did not know anything about those occasions. I then realized that all this happened after she was married, so I'm going to relate here something of those family gatherings.

While Dadda was alive, Christmas was the main event of the year. Every member of the family who was in Shanghai, and their families if they were married, attended. Some close friends were also invited. It was Dad who decided who should be invited. There were so many present that the dining room table stretched all the way into the parlour. The Great Eastern Hotel (which was part of the Wing On Company) catered for these luncheons. It was a real Western meal with turkey, plum pudding and all the trimmings. That was the one day of the year that Dadda celebrated with the whole family.

After Dad passed away, we carried on this family tradition. As the families grew bigger, we started having a Santa Claus as well as the Christmas tree. With Santa Claus himself distributing the gifts, the children were so happy and excited. We made it a rule only to give presents to the younger generation, and just to watch their delight made the occasion more festive than ever. Once I was sitting beside two of my nieces, I believe they were Lenora and Gloria, who said, "Isn't it strange, Santa Claus is wearing the same pants as my father!"

WARTIME SHANGHAI

THE LUCERNE ROAD house was sold in 1943, and the next Christmas luncheon was held in my Wuyi Road house, as Mum was then living with me. Gradually family members had left Shanghai but as a rule whoever remained still got together on Christmas Day. Eventually only part of Pearlie's and my families were left, so Pearlie asked me over to her house and I made the Christmas cake.

The Christmas after Pearlie had passed away, for old times' sake, I asked Jeffrey and Ella to have a Christmas dinner with Mae and me at the Blue Village restaurant. The menu was excellent but as luck would have it Jeffrey had a bad cold and did not attend. The next year when even Jeffrey had gone, I asked Ella to have dinner with us at the same restaurant, and she took her sister along to keep her company. Then Mae left for the States so that was the end of celebrating Christmas for me.

BIRTHDAYS

DAD DID NOT believe in celebrating birthdays. Whenever I reminded him that my birthday was due he would say, "Remember your mother." It wasn't until my nineteenth birthday, the year I was to graduate from McTyeire high school, that I had a party. It was also my Big Chinese Birthday, as I would be twenty according to the lunar calendar. I told Dadda I'd like to have a birthday party for my classmates. Somehow I managed to persuade him to agree, and I invited all my classmates and our supervising teacher, Miss Lester. There were two tables, catered by the Great Eastern Hotel, and after lunch I had a fresh cream birthday cake. After lunch, we walked back to school and I was so happy that Dad had finally let me celebrate my birthday.

As the younger generation grew older it became a Must to celebrate their birthdays. They were usually given a tea party, and as the cousins all played together these also became very happy events. As for the grown-ups, we also celebrated each other's birthdays. Attending birthday parties became a very busy routine. I had to keep a notebook to remind me which birthday was to be celebrated next.

After I married Y.H., his mother's immediate family, the Lius of Foochow, also celebrated my birthday. Since there wasn't room in my house, I used to divide my birthday parties, celebrating April 2nd with the Kwoks and my Chinese birthday, the twelfth day of the second moon, with the Liu relatives. My lunar birthday actually fell on a leap second moon, so when there was a leap second moon I would celebrate both. That meant I'd have three birthday parties instead of just one. (There won't be another leap second moon until I am 95, as it only occurs every 19 years.)

My son, Leonard Zhong Zheng Woo, was born in October 1943, the 17th grandchild of my parents. The others were seven girls and ten boys. In China, baby boys are all called "Didi". When my son was born, my eldest brother, Percy said, "Let's not have another one called Didi."

"Then what should I call him?" I asked.

He thought for a moment and then said, "Deedums."

So even today my son is known to all the family members and relatives as Deedums.

I had wanted to name him after my second brother, Leon. However, I thought Leo was better but then found out that a distant relative had a son called Leo and I did not like that boy, so I named our son Leonard. When my brother asked why I had added the "nard" to his name, I told him because I thought it sounded nicer.

I left the choice of a Chinese name to my husband. He named him Wu Zhongzheng, a name which was easy to write. My husband told me he had difficulty writing his name when he was a child and he did not want his son to have such a problem. However, Zhongzheng was also the name of Chiang Kai-shek, so when liberation came I was rather uneasy about that. People paid more attention to such things, especially later during the Cultural Revolution, so I decided that something had to be done about it.

I told a friend my problem and he suggested that I add elements to the two characters of my son's given name. This made no change in the pronunciation but gave a good meaning to the name. By the time Deedums finished middle school he was using his new Chinese name.

Deedums was only 14 when his father was arrested. He had just finished junior middle school and had passed the exams for the senior school and knew his father would be proud of him and wanted to let him know. So we wrote a short note and took it to the Detention House, but we had no way of knowing whether his father ever received it. I started to mark every day on the calendar after my husband was arrested on March 15, 1958. But after three months I gave up, always wondering what the outcome would be.

Deedum had finished the three years of senior middle school and was now preparing for college. He was a good student and his classmates who also intended to take the exams would come to him for help with their studies.

When the exams took place, and realizing that he was feeling very jittery about the results, I sent him to Beijing to visit his sister. He was not accepted by the university but he had half expected it as he knew his family background was against him. He was determined to get a college education, however, so he stayed home reviewing all the courses he had studied, in addition to taking part in all the manual labour activities required of him because of his background. (It was much later that I found out he even had to push "honey carts" in the early mornings.) In 1962, he took the exams again and this time it was scholastic standing and not family background that counted and he was accepted.

He graduated from Tongji University but according to new rules, graduates had to participate in manual labour for one year before being assigned a job. He was sent to Fengyang, the poorest county of Anhui province, to work in a printing factory. Not one year but ten years passed and he was still working as a labourer; the authorities had forgotten all about him.

Deedums had a college classmate who was also assigned to the printing factory, a real go-getter. He managed to get then both transferred to the Construction Bureau of Fengyang. Although Deedums' education was not in architecture, he was soon drawing blueprints and supervising buildings that were being constructed. Once when I asked how he managed this he told me: "Where there's a will, there's a way."

One day his friend announced that he was going to visit the Technical College in Hefei, the capital of Anhui Province, as he wanted to borrow some books. Deedums asked him to see if he could get some for him too. When his friend showed the list to the college staff, they wanted to know who could read those technical books, so he told them his friend, Z.Z. Woo, could. They were interested and suggested that Woo should pay them a visit. Deedums went along and the head gave him a book and asked him to translate a section into English. He had no difficulty in doing so, even though in both high school and college he had studied Russian, not English.

I might mention here that while in Fengyang, Deedums wrote me weekly letters in English. I corrected them and sent them back to him. At the same time, he kept up with his studies in engineering, etc. The Technical College was impressed and suggested that he work for them. He was only too willing to do so and asked them to notify the Construction Bureau where he was then working. But "No," they said, the Bureau must release him first. When he approached the Bureau to release him, they said they could only do so if the College offered him the job first. Neither wanted to take the first step.

Then a new government policy came down. If a person wished to study for a master's degree, the organization they worked for could not stop them. Deedums' friends advised him to take the exams to enter the graduate college. At first he hesitated as he was afraid that having stopped studying for almost ten years, he would not be able to pass the exams. They persuaded him to try, however, and he passed.

In two years, he had completed the course and was thinking of going abroad for his doctorate. But he was told that after getting his master's degree, he must do manual labour for a year before applying for a job. He finally went to Beijing to put his case before the Bureau of Education. Didn't his ten years of manual labour in Fengyang count? With the help of Hefei Technical College which wanted him to return and teach there when he received his doctorate, he was finally allowed to go to the USA, appointed by the government but self-supported.

CRIME

NO MATTER WHICH country you live in you will find there are always cases of robbery, thieving, kidnapping and murder. I've had my share of those experiences while living in Shanghai.

A friend of mine, Helen Tsang, had returned from New York. We hadn't seen each other since she left Shanghai while we were classmates in high school. That was in 1927 and it was now 1935. I thought Helen had become quite Bohemian; she dressed differently, used black nail polish and painted the tips of her nails green. She suggested that we open a dress salon. She had studied dress designing in New York so she would design the gowns and I was to be the salon manager. We rented a room in the Park Hotel and set up our studio. We called it "Tsingyi." This sounded like her Chinese name, but it wasn't the same two characters. These two characters meant "Brocaded Rainbow." We used only Chinese materials and our main clientele was foreign tourists visiting China. We assured our clients that Helen's designs were for each individual customer and also guaranteed that no two gowns would be the same.

We scouted all the silk shops in the city searching for materials. We learned a lot about Shanghai, finding treasures in small shops in the most unexpected lanes or alleys. Then we planned to go to Hangchow, one of the chief silk manufacturing cities in China. There we hoped to buy some gowns made for the officials of the Ching Dynasty. Helen was good at using these gowns to make modern evening gowns. Hangchow had so much to offer. It was just a matter of being able to locate what we needed.

A friend of my husband was taking his girlfriend to Hangchow for a holiday and invited us to share his car. It was so much nicer traveling by car, but the door on the left-hand side of the front seat had something wrong with it and it couldn't be opened from the outside. Each time I got in I complained that it was such a nuisance and told him he should have it fixed. Y.H. drove, as he was familiar with the roads and Helen and I sat in the front with him. Arriving at Hangchow we left the couple and went about our purchases, meeting them the next day for the homeward trip.

It was already dusk when we started back. As we drew near to Shanghai we came to a bridge. When the car reached the top of the slope I noticed some men waving for us to stop. I thought they were the police wishing to inspect the car but then I noticed one of them was holding a gun and they were not dressed in police uniforms. Our friend in the back seat called out, "Drive on Y.H., I believe this is a hold-up!" Before Y.H. could step on the gas, one of the men tried to open the door but it would not open. I thanked my lucky stars it was out of order; this was one time I did not complain. We started to drive off but the bandits were infuriated and fired at us. I had my face pressed against the windshield when the bullet went through the glass.

Luckily the glass was bulletproof and there was only a small hole, but the glass splinters hit my face. I looked at Helen and cried, "You are bleeding!" She looked at me and said, "You are dripping blood!"

The bandits fired two more shots after us but we were already out of their range. We picked up speed and headed for the nearest hospital as soon as we reached Shanghai. I had 23 cuts on my face; the glass splinters had to be removed, but otherwise no serious damage was done. The bullet had passed over my head and gone out through the ceiling of the car.

Then we felt hungry and went to Jimmy's Kitchen for a bite. While there, I had a brain wave: Here was a chance to get some publicity for our Tsingyi Salon. I telephoned all the English newspapers in town and asked if they wanted a story, if so come over to Jimmy's Kitchen and get it. Next morning we were in print with a picture of the car and arrows pointing to the bullet holes, and of course mentioning Tsingyi dress salon at the Park Hotel.

We also had another experience with kidnappers. My sister's family had taken a cottage in Mokansan for the summer months and she had taken our mother with her. Different members of the Kwok family would take turns visiting them on the weekends. That weekend my sister-in-law Dora, Y.H., and I decided to go. We spent a day or two in Mokansan and then started on our homeward journey. The house was on the top of the hill and we had left the car at the foot. I started running down the path, gathered too much momentum and tripped. My knee was bleeding when we got into the car and Dora suggested that we stop at Hangchow and have it attended to, but I did not think it was serious and did not want to waste time by stopping.

When we reached our old home on Lucerne Road where my brothers and their families now lived, the wound had festered. I showed it to my eldest brother, Percy, and he insisted I should have it cleaned immediately, and he would do it himself. It was always the family custom to have dinner together every evening at eight in the dining room. Percy called the houseboy and gave instructions that dinner was not to be served until he had attended to my leg. This saved the family from the would-be kidnapping. Here is what happened:

The houseboy suddenly appeared and said in Pidgin English, "Master, bad man have come."

Percy immediately turned off the light, locked the door and

45

told us all to lie down on the floor. Then he started phoning the other members of the family (we had five phones in that house). Next he turned on the burglar alarm. The British Settlement police arrived within three minutes. In the meantime, being curious, Wally walked out to his porch and saw some men walking along the corridor which passed our mother's room. He called out, "Who are you?"

Receiving no answer, he fired a shot into the air. That started the fireworks. The kidnappers opened fire and tried running across the lawn to escape. By then the police had arrived and the kidnappers had fled. Only one was caught, the lookout man at the entrance to Lucerne Road. But one pedestrian who was taking an evening stroll was killed by a stray bullet. The kidnappers must have known that at 8:00 p.m. the whole family would be gathered in the dining room. It was my leg that saved my brothers, as the room was empty when the kidnappers broke in at exactly eight o'clock.

Dora was the most frantic during the time the kidnappers were roaming around the house. Her younger son, Donald, then a small baby, was asleep on the third floor and she was so afraid they would find him there. However, after they had left and we unlocked the doors we found that the only thing they had taken was a ten yuan note I had left on Dora's bed in her room. It was there because we had been arguing about who should pay for the gasoline for the trip to Mokanshan and Dora refused to accept the money, so I had left it on her bed.

The next day we decided that we must show our appreciation to our servants for their loyalty to the family. We planned to give them a feast. Then we realized that we didn't even know how many servants there were. A count was made and found there were 24 of them. Two tables of food were ordered from the Great Eastern Hotel for a banquet for them.

CRIME

Not long afterwards, the Lucerne Road Gate was blocked, and a new entrance was built on Great Western Road (now called Yenan Road). The grounds covered eight acres of land and the road leading to the new gate passed the lawns where we had two tennis courts, opposite which was the squash court Julie had given Wally, then by the pond which we once used as a swimming pool, and above which was a summer house on a small hill. The road then curved to pass the hard tennis court and then the hot house and vegetable garden and so-called nursery where Dad used to raise his seedlings etc. The new gate was opposite Dr. K.C. Sun's Maternity Home where Lollie and Deedums were born.

Another incident of this sort took place in my Wuyi Road house. Mum was staying with us, and Julie's amah from Kunshan had recommended her niece Wei-Fen to be Mum's maid. After Mum passed away, I let Wei-Fen stay on to work for me. The wife of Lewis Mason, a Tsinghua classmate of Y.H. and W.S., was murdered when thieves broke into her house while she was alone. They cut the telephone wire and escaped. This case was much talked about because the couple were well known and everyone was so shocked at the news. Y.H. and I talked about it too, not noticing that Wei-Fen was all ears.

Then one day I sent her to Elsie's apartment to change some U.S. dollars into Chinese currency. She remarked that we got such a large sum for them. Well, not long after that our family was going to Y.H.'s Third Uncle's place to celebrate his 60th birthday. The older generation followed all their old feudalistic customs and the younger generation had to spend two days celebrating their birthdays, especially the BIG ones. So I started dressing Lollie for the occasion and then realized that she did not have any red clothing. It would never do for her to appear in white or blue, so I decided we'd go out and buy something suitable.

47

In no time we returned with a pretty red blouse. As we got to the gate I noticed it wasn't locked, then when we entered I found my safety strong box on the steps leading to the front door. Beside it was a cloth bundle in which my jewels were wrapped. We immediately entered the front door, which was also unlocked, and called Wei-Fen. No answer.

I rushed up the stairs and noted the contents of my redwood cupboard on the top landing were spilled on the floor. Then I heard Wei-Fen calling out. She said she was locked in the bathroom. I happened to have a second set of keys, so I immediately opened the door and found her with her hands tied together (very loosely). She said the robber had raped her then locked her in the bathroom with a string from the blind.

I went to the phone to call Y.H., but found the wires had been cut so I went next door to use their phone. Next, I called the police. They soon arrived and got Wei-Fen to tell them exactly what had happened. She said there were two robbers and even described the clothes they wore. After one of them had raped her, they locked her in the bathroom and she knew nothing more. When she first told me she had been raped, I asked her where did it happen, she said on my bed. However, I noticed my bed was as smooth as a freshly made one, so I wondered!

By this time, Y.H. had returned and our houseboy Soong Ling had returned from having a haircut that he told us Wei-Fen had insisted he go and have. The police decided to take Wei-Fen to the police station for further questioning and I drove them there. The police informed me that there were no signs of her having been raped, but she was already pregnant.

While we were at the police station, Y.H. had connected the telephone wire and phoned to say he suspected Wei-Fen, and to be sure to ask the police to escort us home as he did not think it safe to have Wei-Fen alone with me in the car. Y.H. had searched

Wei-Fen's room and the toilet next door and in the toilet tank had found the U.S. dollars. The police decided to take Wei-Fen to the police station for the night, and to investigate further. She came back next morning as cheerful as ever not realising what we had found. We told her she would have to leave.

After reviewing the case, we came to the conclusion as to how everything happened. It seems that Wei-Fen was having an affair with the son of Percy's old employee, Mr. Feng. When she discovered she was pregnant, they planned the robbery. She remembered our discussing the other case where the telephone wires were cut so she did the same. She had gathered all the loot, cash, jewellery and other valuables and was ready to flee when Lollie and I suddenly returned. She had thought we were going straight to the birthday celebration. When she heard us, she rushed to the bathroom, locked the door and tied her hands together. Later I found the key under some towels in the bathroom.

We never learned what happened to young Mr. Feng and what part he actually played. However, just recently I asked Soong Ling to tell me all he knew and remembered. He said he had heard her making a phone call to Feng telling him the police had discovered what had happened. Then she said "Tell me what do you intend to do? Do you still want me? If you do, I won't involve you but take the blame myself." Evidently he agreed, as later on they lived together.

I was rather amused by the newspaper report of the case. They blamed the capitalistic atmosphere that Wei-Fen lived in that prompted her to commit the crime. It made me feel that I was to blame. So much for thieves and robbers!

Leon later wrote about Dadda and a work-related incident. I'd like to add here that Dad had to wear a bullet-proof vest and carry a gun. The vest was very heavy and uncomfortable to wear, but he felt he had to. Coming home at night, he would sit tensely in the car with his pistol in hand ready to shoot if held up. One day, the car went over a big bump in the road and Dad accidentally pulled the trigger – luckily it was aimed downward. After that Dad decided he would rather relax and not have his pistol in his hand.

LEARNING TO DRIVE

IN THE BEGINNING we had only one car, a Buick. After driving Dad to the office it would return home for Mum to use and then in the evening go back for Dad. Eventually Dad decided to get another car and he would drive it himself. Then Mum could use the car with the chauffeur. But then Dad did not find it so convenient to drive himself, so he announced that he would use the chauffeur, and whoever could drive could use the second car.

Dad was full of verve. He took driving lessons and when he decided to carry a pistol he took shooting lessons. Elsie was quick to take advantage of this. She accompanied Dad to his lessons and took lessons herself. And in no time she could drive and handle a pistol as well.

One day in 1928, while I was recuperating from a serious case of typhoid fever, Elsie told me she was going to teach me to drive, then together we would get more chances to use the second car. I protested as I was not a daredevil like Elsie, who could ride, drive, swim and shoot. But she put me in the car and explained what I was to do. I was so weak I didn't even have enough strength in my legs to push the clutch down, not to mention the brakes. But Elsie persuaded me to practice hard and keep on trying and eventually she decided to take me out on the road. I'm no good at directions and so I just followed her instructions. Finally we got on a road that had a creek in front of it. Elsie said "Turn around and go back". I was in a panic as I didn't know how to make a U-turn and so I aimed at the creek.

Luckily Elsie grabbed the steering wheel and was able to point the car in the right direction.

Then Elsie decided I was to take a driving test. I knew I wasn't ready but she was adamant and she then arranged everything. I sat at the wheel with the British policeman beside me. When we reached a red light, he said "Stop". I did so, but I didn't even know how to put the gear in neutral. He did so for me and then when we were ready to go again, he told me to go back to first gear. I passed and got a driving license – don't ask me how.

One day Elsie said we should take a longer drive and go to Minhang. She took the wheel and I was breathless at the speed she drove. "Don't worry", she told me, "This is like a highway. You are supposed to speed."

Suddenly in the distance I saw a car speeding towards us.

"Road Hog", said Elsie, and stepped on the gas. "I'll teach him a lesson!"

As the two cars almost reached each other they both swerved and stopped; it was Wally in the other car.

Two of a kind, I thought.

THE BLACK MARIA

I'M NO GOOD at remembering exact dates but it was during the time when the Japanese occupied the outskirts of Shanghai that this incident took place. Shanghai was still very much under the influence of the foreigners at that time. There was the International Settlement governed by the British and the French Concession ruled by the French. The suburbs or outskirts, however, were not under their jurisdiction and gambling dens cropped up like mushrooms there. These places were crowded every night; I believe all Chinese love gambling and my family was no exception. We just could not resist visiting these gambling parlours, usually to end up losing much more than we had intended.

Eventually rumours were circulating that people were being robbed or even murdered while on their way to the gambling districts. We then took the precaution of attending less frequently. Then one day a Russian croupier approached my husband and told him how he had noticed we were interested in roulette and that he was planning to operate a roulette table in his home, only for a small select group. We knew it was against the law to open such an establishment in the Settlement, but it did not take him much effort to persuade us it would be perfectly safe. We were so gullible, especially my husband. He even arranged to lend the croupier the chips (counters) needed for the game.

The opening date was set and that evening we gathered at the appointed place. We had made sure to arrive separately so as not to arouse suspicion. The long roulette table was set up in the front room, surrounded by chairs. We took our places and began to place our bets. Each roulette player has his own system of betting. Some played the middle section, others played high or low numbers, etc. My system was to follow a certain number.

That evening I chose number 8. I placed chips on 8, 18 and 28 and waited for the wheel to spin. Each time my numbers did not appear, I'd double my bets. It seemed luck was against me but I persevered, deciding I'd quit only when my last chip was gone. By then the three numbers were piled high with my chips. The croupier spun the wheel again and I watched breathlessly as each time the ball passed one of my numbers. The wheel stopped and the ball dropped into number 8. I rose from my chair and shouted, "I'm home!" meaning I had won at last.

At practically the same moment the door burst open and in came several British Municipal Police.

"Don't move," one of them ordered. "You are all under arrest."

Next we were told to file out of the house and get into the black vehicle parked outside. I had never seen such a car before.

"What is it?" I asked. "Where are we going?"

I was told we were going to the police station and the car was called a "Black Maria", an official vehicle used to carry arrested individuals to the police station or to prison. We got in and it started off with the sirens blaring all along the route.

Arriving at the police station we were ushered into a room where they started taking our fingerprints, just as though we were real criminals. Then they told us we would be held on bail for five hundred dollars each. We looked at each other in bewilderment, not knowing what was going to happen next. Then one member of our group managed to get permission to use the telephone. We had to notify our families of the predicament we were in. The waiting seemed endless. When the phone rang we listened attentively to see if it was news for us. If the door opened we jumped up expectantly, hoping it was someone we knew, or if help was coming.

It was way past midnight when the door opened again and one of my brothers walked in. We were so relieved to see him. He paid the bail for our family group. Before we were allowed to leave we had to give our names and write down where we lived. We knew quite well that this was going to be a headline story in the morning papers, so we all gave fictitious names and addresses.

As a sequel to this incident, let me tell you how, so late at night, our brother managed to raise the cash to bail us out. He finally got in touch with his brother-in-law who was the manager of a movie theatre. Our brother then persuaded him to let us use the money from the day's sale of tickets. Luckily it was enough to cover the bail for all our family members who were under arrest. The morning papers did carry the story, but I don't think many of our friends were fooled by the fictitious names, as we were the butt of their jokes for a long time afterwards.

CAPITALIST

THEN LIBERATION came and eventually the German members of our firm had to leave Shanghai. Private firms then became "Joint Private/Government" organizations. I had started working in Transmarina in 1954 and I was asked by some staff members to help with the correspondence. Formerly all letters were written in German by the German members, but according to the new rules they had to be done in English. They used to telephone me and ask me to correct over the phone a letter they had written. I thought it would be easier if I just dropped in at the office instead.

I had had no training in writing business letters, but after reading a few books I decided I could at least make myself understood. I used to go in for a few hours a day whenever I found it convenient as I was only helping out and did not intend that this work would interfere with my household duties. Then the staff decided I should receive a salary, and after a while they told me they had sent my name to the labor union and I was now considered a regular member of the firm. Next I was informed that my working hours were eight hours a day, with an extra hour of political study every morning. In order to skip the political study periods, I decided to join the Chinese classes which were run by the firm.

Then the next step was that the Joint Enterprises became fully State Organizations and I was assigned to the China National Import Export Corporation as an English secretary. After that, I was assigned to the China National Scientific Instruments

Corporation, where I had to learn to write export letters.

My husband was working as one of the heads of the Instrument Corporation. Our old firm Transmarina Scientific Supplies continued to use our old name to correspond with our German firms. But my husband was arrested in 1958 during the Anti-Rightist Movement. He was put in a detention house waiting for his sentence. I was at the school on Changshu Road where the capitalists of the foreign trade corporations were sent to have their brains washed, when I was told I should immediately return home. It was March 15th, 1958. When I got there I found the police were waiting for me. They informed me Y.H. Woo was arrested and I was to prepare some clothes, bedding, toilet articles, etc., to take to him. I was in a daze and waited for Deedums to return from school and together we began to pack the things.

Before we left the house, I received a strange phone call. The person phoning just told me where Y.H.'s car was parked. (Actually I knew where it was, but I never found out who had telephoned me.) After we had delivered the clothes, we went to look for the car. It was in very bad condition. Perhaps Y.H. had known this and I imagined that perhaps he was hoping to have an accident while driving. I had begged him many times not to use a car as no capitalists did at that time, but he was stubborn. I was already taking buses to work. I drove the car back and somehow by stopping and drawing to the curb every time the engine rattled, I finally managed to get it home. That was the last time I drove a car. When we got back home, Didi said "Mummy, today I have grown up."

I was teaching English in the School of Foreign Trade. I was ready to retire but someone said they wanted to start oral English classes.

"Now, who can speak English here?"

And some smart aleck said "Daisy". I told the secretary to say I was sick, so every week the telephone call would come and I would tell the secretary to say I was sick or absent. But one day she said, "There's nothing I can do, it's the Party Secretary and you can't refuse him!" So I said okay. I went to the school where I was supposed to train Communist Party members to go abroad. All the capitalists in foreign trade, 650 of us, were sent to Chung Ming Island. I remember one member saying to me that when the Americans arrived, he and I could act as interpreters. I said, look, if I report those words you're going to be killed.

Every eight weeks, they would send new cadres down. Some were nice but some would try to be as mean as they could to us. One day I buttoned my coat by mistake onto my Chairman Mao badge and I had a hundred fingers pointed at me. So everything has a funny side to it.

In 1971, the ten oldest members were allowed to go home. My house was in Wuyi Road. I had bought a house on borrowed land, meaning that when the date is up, you either buy the land or give it back to the landowner. It was just one *mu* of land and the owner would say three, and we'd take the bars over and he'd say "Who said three? I said six." "All right, we'll give him six." "What made you think it was six? It was ten." It went on like that, and then after liberation came – to Hell with him. So he came around and asked me to give him *anything*. I said, "Sorry, I don't have anything to give you." So when the ten years was up, I just gave it to the government.

After Y.H.'s arrest, the leader of our corporation told me I was to change my work. I was sent to the Foreign Trade Farm in Kiangwan. Since I had a young son at home, I received special treatment and was allowed to return home every day instead of living at the farm. This was no easy task as it took two buses and one-and-a-half hours to get there; I had to leave the house at 5:00

a.m.

On the farm I did all sorts of manual labor, grew vegetables, raised pigs and built pig sties, but mainly I acted as a "small" helper to the masons or workers who were building larger buildings on the farm. I mixed cement, carried it to them and passed up bricks, one by one, after soaking them in water. I also did odd jobs. During the period of the Three Years of Natural Calamities when food was hard to get, I was asked to stop on my way home after work and deliver eggs to the heads of the Customs office. I had to collect payment for the eggs and one day, I short-changed them by two cents unintentionally, and when I found out I had to make another trip to refund the two cents. Another job was to give the hogs that we used for breeding an egg each and every day. They were so big, they terrified me. When they saw me approaching their pen they would stand on two feet, lean against the fence and open their mouths while I threw the eggs in.

The most difficult time I had while working on this farm was during the Great Leap Forward. At times we worked until 10:00 p.m. but had to be back at the farm the next morning at 7:00 a.m. I did not get much sleep during those days and often fell asleep hanging on to a strap in the bus as it was seldom that I could get a seat. Once a worker also fell asleep and rested his head on my shoulder as he also hung onto a strap. I just did not have the heart to tell him to stand on his own feet. Another time I slept so soundly that I did not wake up when the bus arrived at the station where I was to get off. When I did wake up I didn't know where I was and had to find my way home.

Another assignment was to peel off the outer layer of leaves of huge white (Chinese) cabbages which came from the north. They were to be exported to Hong Kong and the frozen leaves had to be removed before they were packed again. The work site was the South Wharf so I had to take a bus there every morning. In spite of my wearing cotton gloves covered by a woolen pair and finally by a rubber pair, my fingers would be frozen stiff when I finished the day's work. This caused the arthritis I suffer from now. My fingers are disfigured and I can't grasp things tightly. Thank heavens I suffer no pain, only stiffness.

Once every month, I was allowed to take things to the detention house for Y.H., but no food. The only way I knew he was alive was to see his signature on the receipt for the goods. He begged me to bring medicine for his asthma. When I took the medicine on my next trip there, the guards refused to accept it. They said the [Ward Road] prison hospital could take care of him.

Y.H. died in the D-Lei-Jiao [Ward Road] prison hospital on December 11, 1961, without our ever seeing him again since the day he was arrested in March 1958. I was notified the next day while I was at the farm, and told to go to the detention house immediately. When I got there, they gave me the news and asked if I had any requests. I asked why they did not notify me earlier so that I could have at least seen him alive. They said they did not know where I was. Such a LIE. I told them I wanted my son to see his father's body. They took me home but told me I was to tell my son that he must not cry. I told my son this and he replied, "You need not worry, I certainly will not cry for them to see."

When we arrived at the morgue the body was brought out for us to view. Except for the clothes it was beyond recognition, so thin it seemed he had starved to death. I touched his arm but could only feel a bone, no flesh. I covered his face with my handkerchief and we left.

Right after Y.H.'s death I was transferred to the "Li-Tung Hui", known as the directors' office. I thought this was one step before retirement. But luck was not with me; the Foreign Trade Spare Time College was going to start a class in oral English and someone had suggested that I should teach there. Whenever the phone calls came I told the secretary to say I wasn't there as I had absolutely no experience in teaching English. The calls kept coming and eventually I had to accept after the Party Secretary called me.

When I got to the school I was told to audit Teacher Li's classes and learn from him, but I went one better. I not only consolidated his good points but made my own method of teaching which seemed to meet the approval of the students. Little did I realize that I was causing Teacher Li to dislike me. He was jealous, especially when his students wanted to drop out of his class in order to join mine.

Y.H.'s sentence came down in September 1962 and I was informed by the court that I was responsible for the fines. He was labelled a counter-revolutionary, was accused of misappropriating government funds and of possessing weapons. The fine was 130,000 RMB or US$64,000.

I asked the court how I was supposed to raise these sums as my salary was only 158 RMB and I had to live. They had already confiscated everything of value that I owned. This included, cash, jewellery, clothing, furniture and even my children's brass beds. They said this did not cover the fines and I still owed them 140,000 RMB. They said I should consult my leaders. I immediately went back to the Foreign Trade Spare Time College where I was teaching but was told by the Party Member Principal that they were not my leaders; I did not belong to the school as they had only borrowed me from the China National Machine Corporation and those were my leaders.

I then went to the Corporation and asked to see the head of the personnel department. Some young workers there told me the head had no time to see me so to tell them what I wanted. I insisted on seeing the head but they said she was at a meeting.

They told me to leave my name and they would contact me by phone to give me an appointment. I waited and waited, but nothing happened, so I tried phoning her instead. She said she did not know me, and was too busy anyway, but she would call me again when she was free. Again I waited in vain, and then came the Four Clean-Ups Movement and I was made one of the targets of this movement.

The Four Clean-Ups Movement took place in 1964. Since I was the only capitalist in the department besides Charlie Ma, I was made the target. A Working Group came from Beijing to help our school conduct the movement. They did not know anything about me nor could they pin anything on me, so they held my husband's wrong-doings against me. They said: "The good man has died but you were the brains behind his crimes, and you have survived." The slogan was, "Confess all and you will be treated leniently." Before long I realized that was exactly what they wanted me to do – confess my sins.

At the beginning of the movement, meetings were held every day in each department of the school. Classes were suspended and each teacher would give a talk accusing me of my crimes. This is where Eddy Li showed his true colors. He was a good talker and dramatically accused me of things which were only partly true, but by the time he had embellished his stories it seemed he actually convinced the other teachers that I was as bad as he had made me out to be. All the teachers had to say something about me. I realize now that if they did not they would be accused of trying to defend me, which made them as bad as I was.

At first, I tried to defend myself by explaining why I had done certain things but the more I explained the worse my crimes became. In the end I gave up, accepted the accusations, admitted my wrongdoings as I had thought too much of myself instead of others, wanted to continue my capitalist way of life, live in comfort, etc. I then admitted that my thoughts were all wrong, and not in accordance with the government policy. I had to change.

Every afternoon, two members of our department, one a party member, would take me to a small room for a few hours grilling. I was told to confess all. Then in the evenings I had to write down all I had said and hand in the statement the next day. They would ask me to relate things that I knew nothing about. If I said I did not know, they accused me of lying or of refusing to confess. This went on day after day. Once I went to the clinic to get some medicine. The doctor sensed that I was under a strain. He was sympathetic and gave me some tranquilizers. I took two pills instead of one, and actually found myself falling asleep during the afternoon questioning. No more tranquilizers for me!

In the evenings the teachers held meetings to decide how to run the movement. I was not allowed to participate as they were probably deciding how to deal with *me*. I was put in a small room by myself. When the meetings were over, I was told to go home. One evening I seemed to have sat in the small room for hours without being told I could leave. Finally I ventured out only to find the place in pitch darkness except for the room where a cadre on duty sat. I must have startled him when I appeared.

"What are you doing here?" he demanded.

I told him I was waiting for permission to leave when the meeting was over.

"It ended long ago," he said. "You'd better go home."

They had forgotten all about me!

When I got home at night I would get out my typewriter and begin to draft the required article. Sometimes I wanted to rebel and refuse to write, but Didi would tell me, "Mummy, you have to write, go on and finish your writing." I'd grit my teeth and write and write.

Once they held a big meeting with over a hundred people present to accuse me of my crimes. I sat in front facing the group while different members got up to talk. The things they accused me of were so fantastic that I began enjoying listening to them. Here is one that amused me. This teacher said that when I went shopping at the Wing On Department Store, I went directly up to the office on the 5th floor and had the attendants bring up the merchandise I wished to have. The goods were brought up in trays and they paraded it in front of me as I reclined on a leather sofa with a cup of tea in one hand and a cigarette in the other and just pointed to the things I wanted. They said I didn't even pay for them. I thought I was listening to a story from the *Arabian Nights*. So much for that movement.

After Y.H. was arrested, it seemed that any time there was a movement for manual labor I was always one of the first to be picked to participate. During the movement to produce steel from scrap iron, I was sent off for three months. All day, I had to break rocks and large stones into small pieces. At times, my son would drop by to help me break up some of the large pieces that I could not handle.

Another time, I was sent to Xing Tsong to pick chrysanthemums for tea. This was not hard work, but I was also assigned to clean the toilets as well. Cleaning toilets seems to be the communist method of meting out punishment. I can't keep track of the number of toilets I have cleaned. I recall the first time was in 1958 when all capitalists of the Foreign Trade Corporations were sent to a school to have our brains washed. We had to take turns keeping the toilets clean. When my turn came I didn't even know how to wring out a mop and made a mess of everything. The first thing I did when I got home was to ask my maid to teach me to wring a mop dry.

During the Four Clean-Up Movement it was again my task

to clean the women's toilet in the school. I had to go before the morning classes started and the teachers had arrived. The worst part was to have the children who lived on the floors below follow me and try to tell me what to do, or telling me to do it all over again, that I hadn't made things clean enough. I learned from experience not to argue with anyone but to just go ahead and carry out their instructions – or at least I pretended to.

Cleaning toilets in the countryside was a much harder and dirtier job. In the city, we had flush toilets but at the farms and other places where I was sent to do manual labor, toilets were nothing but a large hole dug in the ground, and my job was to carry wooden commodes from the women's dormitory and empty them. Then I had to go to the creek and wash the commode and carry it back to the dormitory.

Just before Y.H.'s sentence came down, I was sent to Tsingpu to dig fish ponds. The women members slept in a shack where ducks were originally kept. Straw was laid on the damp ground and our bedding was laid on top of it. In the morning, the straw was damp and we had to carry it outside to dry it as best we could. There were eight of us in this small shack and we were so cramped that we could hardly turn over at night without disturbing the person sleeping beside us.

Our makeshift dormitory was by a stream. When I asked where I was to get water to wash my face and brush my teeth, I was told to get water from the creek as the country folk did. I carried my wash basin to the bank of the stream and looked down. People were washing clothes, others were washing vegetables, but what shocked me was to see farther up the stream some were washing their wooden commodes. For three days I just refused to wash. I was told that even our drinking water came from that same stream but alum was put in to purify it.

How My House Was
Searched After
Y.H.'s Arrest

THE FIRST TIME was a few days after he was taken to the detention house. They opened my locked drawers where I kept my cash, jewellery, and bank deposit slips. They confiscated all this as well as some government bonds I had received as part of my salary. Next they moved my crystal and curio cabinets to a room that I had used as a box room and then they sealed that room. All my winter clothes were in there. I had to get myself another warm jacket and overcoat, each day hoping they would let me have some warmer clothing.

They then began making further searches of my home. Strange as it may seem, they always came at two or three in the morning when it was very dark. I'd hear my watchdog bark and knew they were here again. They came two or three times like this, searching all my belongings, sometimes taking some things, but never mentioning what they were really looking for. Then I gradually caught on. Y.H. was being constantly urged to "confess". He probably mentioned things which gave them a clue. The following case is an example.

We had kept some gold bars and U.S. dollars in a secret part of one of our night tables. After Y.H. was arrested, I removed the contents and asked one of his cousins to keep them for me. She agreed and rolled them in a roll of toilet paper, but after a few weeks she got nervous and told me she couldn't keep them any longer and she gave them back to me. Didi and I put them back in the secret compartment. It was lucky we had, as one night they came and demanded to know where the money was kept. I immediately knew Y.H. had told them. They took it away and Didi and I thanked our lucky stars that we had put it back in time! Heaven knows what would have happened if they found the compartment empty.

As mentioned before, Y.H. was arrested in March 1958 and died in December 1961 but it wasn't until September 1962 that his sentence came down. I was then at Tsingpu, a suburb of Shanghai, doing manual labor digging fish ponds. The leader of our group told me I was to return to Shanghai immediately and let the police know I was there. I took a bus to the city, leaving my bedding and clothes at the fish pond site, thinking I would be returning.

When I reached Shanghai the police told me they would come to my home the next morning and I was to wait there for them. The next morning they came and handed me Y.H.'s sentence, and they had come to confiscate my belongings to cover the amount he was fined. They said that according to the law I was responsible for the fine in spite of the fact that Y.H. was already dead.

First they took my furniture, leaving me only part of my bedroom suite with two beds. Then they opened up my box room which they had sealed in 1958 and removed the cabinets they had moved there and also other furniture in that room. They took everything of value that I kept in the adjoining rooms, beautiful dinner sets, crystals, glasses, carpets, linens, and furs that I had kept in cupboards and camphor wood trunks; the trunks were all beautiful carved ones.

Later I was given a list of the items they had confiscated,

too long to record here, and then they told me I still owed them 140,000 RMB. I asked how they had arrived at such a figure. They said the value of the confiscated items were estimated by a consignment store and showed me the amounts they had given. I asked them to let me have a copy but was refused. Finally the person in charge of the case relented and said I could sit in an outer room and copy the list if I wished. I was surprised to find they had estimated the three-carat diamond ring my father had given me at 400 RMB and my engagement ring at even less. One of the items was estimated at eight cents. I couldn't figure out what it was and then realised they were crystal sticks for mixing cocktails. My two refrigerators were estimated at 400 and 300 RMB.

When I asked whether the estimated value of the goods was rather low, they told me it had been done by one of the best government consignment stores. Did I not trust the government? Of course I could say nothing. So after they had totaled the sum of all the confiscated goods I still owed 140,000 RMB.

Referring again to Y.H.'s sentence, I'll write here about the weapons he was supposed to have possessed. There were three revolvers and some bullets. These had been left in Shanghai by my brothers, Leon and George.

One day, George had come to our house with two revolvers. He was already planning to leave China and did not know what to do with them and asked for our help. I suggested that he turn them over to the authorities but he said he didn't dare. At that time everyone was encouraged to turn in any arms or ammunition they had. But he told me how the manager of the Great Eastern Hotel (Wing On's hotel) had turned in his revolver, and he was arrested and we never heard any more about him. So George said he couldn't afford to take a chance. Y.H. had decided to help him get rid of the guns. One day we drove to an amusement park in the suburbs, hired a boat to row around the lake, and dropped one of the guns in it. The second one we took to Pearl's garden in Hungjao and dropped it in a stream there. With a sigh of relief we returned home.

Now George was ready to leave Shanghai but suddenly he came again with another revolver and some bullets. I asked him where on earth he had got them? Well, he was cleaning out Leon's desk in the Wing On Co. (Leon and his family had left China before liberation) when suddenly out popped a secret drawer, and in it was the gun. He tried but couldn't find the gadget that had opened the drawer so he took the contents out and brought them to us. It was late at night and Y.H. said he'd find some means of getting rid of them, but in the meantime we'd better hide them in our garden. He dug a hole near a tree that was to be our landmark. I stood on the veranda upstairs watching him.

Now this is what happened to two of these revolvers, the second and third ones. The gardens in Hungjao were looted and destroyed by the country folk just before the Communist soldiers arrived in Shanghai. The stream in my sister's garden had dried up and the gun we had thrown there was found and handed over to the authorities. They immediately interrogated my sister and her husband but they knew nothing. They said they had never been there since the gardens were destroyed. When she innocently told me about this, I thanked my lucky stars I had not told her what we had done.

Now for gun number three. When Y.H. was arrested in 1958 and kept in the detention house he was asked to confess his wrongdoings. I've explained before that the method used was: "Confess all and you will be treated leniently." And evidently Y.H. must have confessed about hiding the gun in our garden. One day the security men came with an interpreter. I always insisted my Chinese was limited. They talked to each other while

I looked on innocently and asked what they wanted. He told the interpreter to go ahead.

Q. Have you anything you shouldn't have?
A. I don't understand, what are things I should not have.
(Each time she then asked the other cadre what she should say.)
Q. Things which are unlawful to keep.
A. I don't know what items are unlawful, could you give me an example?
Q. Well, for instance, a gun or something.

Immediately I caught on. Y.H. had confessed.

A. Yes, I believe there was a gun.
Q. Do you know where it is?
A. It's in the garden, would you like to see it?

I gave them a spade, led them to the garden, pointed to "the spot" and said "I think it is buried there, dig and find out." They uncovered the revolver and a box of bullets and asked me to give a written statement. I told them my Chinese wasn't good enough and said I'd write in English, or perhaps they would write it for me. They agreed that I should tell them verbally and they would write a statement which I was to sign. I was then surprised when they read the statement to me. They praised me for co-operating with them and volunteering to help uncover the goods. I never mentioned the other two guns, hoping Y.H. had kept quiet too.

Y.H. must have also confessed to bringing in money from Hong Kong. He never explained to me where it came from, but he used to get me to collect the cash for him. While we were both working in a foreign trade corporation, we used to go to the coffee shop after lunch as it was usually crowded at lunchtime. A stranger (to me) motioned that we could join his table and we did. Then I realised Y.H. knew him. He handed Y.H. a package wrapped in newspaper which Y.H. dropped into my bag. When we left, he told me to give it to him after work when we got home. I insisted on knowing what the contents were and he said he had done some business with this man and this cash was his share of the profits.

From time to time, Y.H. would ask me to meet this man (Mr. S., a Jew) and get the package. I suspected something wasn't quite right, but I followed his instructions. One time I was told to go to the Park Hotel's new restaurant in the penthouse and have lunch with this man. I was a bundle of nerves and could hardly eat. After I had received the package, I couldn't get away fast enough.

After Y.H.'s arrest, I received a phone call from this man to meet him at a certain place after dark. I went, roamed up and down the street at the appointed place but did not see him. Suddenly he appeared out of a doorway, took my arm and said, "Let's go to a nearby restaurant. I'm afraid this spot is being watched." (When I look back, I guess I must have had pretty strong nerves.) I followed him and he gave me the package. He told me he knew Y.H. had been arrested and this was the last package. I never saw him again.

One day, some time afterwards while I was at the office, the security people asked me to go to a separate room as they wished to ask me a few questions. They laid out seven or eight passport-size photographs and asked me if I recognised anyone. I immediately recognised Mr. S., but I picked up each picture and gazed at them one by one and shook my head.

"All foreigners look alike to me," I told them. "I can't distinguish one from the other."

They told me to take my time and look carefully. My brain was twirling around trying to decide what to do.

Then one of them said to the other, "It's already noon, let's continue after lunch." They told me to go and have my lunch and return afterward.

When I got back, the pictures were laid out on the table again in a row. I glanced at them and then noticed a sheaf of papers on the table beside them. I recognised the handwriting. It was Y.H.'s.

Pretending to be looking at the pictures, I read what I could on his written statement. I noticed the words (translated) "only my wife knows about this." I realised Y.H. had confessed.

I looked again at the pictures, appearing to concentrate very hard, and then said, "I really can't tell but this one seems a bit familiar." I picked up Mr S.'s picture.

"What is his name?" they wanted to know.

I told them I couldn't remember names but they told me to think again so I said I thought it began with an S.

"Yes, that's right, now tell us all you know about him."

So I told them the story of how I met him at the coffee shop, and that I understood he was in business with my husband, and how sometimes my husband had asked me to receive a package for him but I never knew what the contents were. They were satisfied with my report and told me I could leave.

THE CULTURAL REVOLUTION

A DOCTOR WHO was the head of a hospital was on his way to work by bus. (Cars were no longer used by capitalists or intellectuals.) Every morning his wife gave him a five-fen coin for his bus fare. She put it in his pocket. Buses are always very crowded and the doctor had to stand. He tried to put his hand into his pocket to get his five-fen coin, but instead he put his hand into the pocket of the passenger standing beside him. The man immediately shouted that there was a pick-pocket on the bus.

The bus stopped and the doctor was taken to the police station. When questioned, he gave his name and the hospital where he worked, and confessed. The Party members of the hospital immediately came to the station to find out what had happened to the head of their hospital. He explained.

"But why didn't you tell the bus conductor?" they asked.

"Because if I had tried to explain, they would not have believed me, and might have even beaten me up. I thought it safer to admit my wrongdoing."

Before the Four Clean-up Movement ended, the Cultural Revolution started. Since I was being treated as a criminal by the teachers of the Spare Time College, I was always alone. No one dared talk to me. After lunch in the mess hall, I used to take a walk. I either wandered along the Bund or else went window shopping on Nanking Road.

This time I felt a difference in the atmosphere. People were rushing here and there when I reached Nanking Road. Near

Honan Road I saw the sign boards of the well-known silk shop Lao Chia Fook being pulled down. They were set on fire right in the middle of the road. The crowds were shouting with glee. This was my first experience of getting rid of the "four olds." Soon I was to learn how the capitalists were to be dealt with.

I was considered a capitalist, so one day I was put in a truck with some Red Guards and members of the school's staff. They drove to the corner of Wuyi Road where I lived and told me to get out. Then we started to walk to my house. Red Guards surrounded me, beating drums and shouting slogans, "Down with the capitalists," etc.

Arriving at my house, they locked me in a small room and began to take away anything they considered were 'four olds', or rather anything that was luxurious in their eyes. They took away most of my belongings or sealed them in my box room. I wasn't even allowed a change of sheets, nor any winter clothing. I was given a maintenance fee of 12 yuan a month, with the same amount for my son, who was then studying at Tung Chi University. He had to pay 15 yuan for his board, so I gave him three from my 12. Then I had to pay for half of my bus monthly tickets, another three yuan so I ended up with six yuan a month.

The first thing I did was to look around and see how I could make ends meet. I immediately cancelled my two phones, then I told my maid I could no longer afford to keep her. She refused to leave and said I had to pay her more than 300 yuan for the 15 years she had worked for me, as a severance fee. If I refused she was going to continue to work and add her monthly salary on the amount I owed her. I consulted with Didi and we decided to sell his camera, one of his most treasured possessions, and which by chance the Red Guards had overlooked. We only got 278 yuan for the camera. How could we make up the balance? I looked around the room and said, "I wonder how much we could get for the portable radio?" She understood some English and said, "I'll accept the radio as the balance." Knowing that it was worth more than that amount, we agreed and I asked her to sign a receipt. Didi was against it, but I insisted.

Not long afterwards, the Red Guards told me to move out of the house. I asked where I was to move to, and they told me the Housing Committee would assign me a place to live. I was given the choice of two places. Both were in what they considered the poorest section of our district.

One was in a yard, just a room with no kitchen, no sanitary conveniences, and water was to be got from a community tap in the yard. Cooking was to be done in the one room, one that was to serve all purposes. The second place was a small room over the kitchen, six square meters in size with a loft overhead. At least there was running water and a flush toilet to be shared with the other two families who occupied the house (one large room each). I went to see my son at his college and told him to help me decide. He chose the second place, so we started moving.

We measured each piece of furniture to see which ones could fit into that tiny room. There was just enough space for my bed, the chefro [a tall wardrobe], a writing desk and a three-cornered cupboard that had been in the bathroom. We also took a small folding table. In the loft we put Didi's bed, a bookcase and a trunk. On top of the chefro, I put what used to be a food cupboard. As Jeffrey said when he saw how we had fixed the room, "You had to build upwards to save space."

As the furniture was being moved in we found the roof was leaking; we could see the sun through the holes in it. A good friend (he was Pearl's handyman) helped us get some cheap second-hand plastic strips and fixed it so that it would keep out the rain. Once Didi said, "I think I'll cut out some stars and paste them on the plastic, and imagine I am sleeping under the sky". I'm glad he had such a cheerful attitude to the whole thing. Anyway, the place was liveable in spite of the many drawbacks. For instance, Didi could not sleep in the loft in the summer — too hot — x and in the winter, the water in my face basin would turn into ice.

The three of us were supposed to live there, me and my son and the maid. Luckily for me, she decided she didn't want to move so she took her name from our residence book and took out her own residence book. She did that for her own benefit, as she had a room to herself fully furnished with my furniture that she had claimed as her own. I was only too glad to get rid of her as I soon found out she did everything for her own advantage. Well, it takes all kinds to make a society.

One day after I had settled in my new room, a stranger came running up the stairs yelling my name. I met him on the landing and asked who he was and what he wanted.

"Don't pretend not to know me," he said, "I've come to collect the money you owe my mother. I am Jing Hua's son (my maid's name). She told me how you mistreated her, moved out and not giving her a cent. I had to go to the police station to find you."

I thanked my lucky stars that I had demanded a receipt from his mother when I paid her the severance fee. I took out the receipt and showed it to him.

"But she swore you never gave her a cent," he said.

"You had better settle with her," I replied, and asked him to leave.

Living on six yuan a month was no easy task, barely enough for food. I did not eat breakfast and had lunch in the school mess hall, always picking the cheapest dish. On my way home, I would drop in at Pearl's and have dinner there. She wasn't much better off than I, but her husband, son and daughter-in-law together had more than I. The Red Guards found out that I was seeing my sister and accused me of making "underground connections." They forbade me to go there again.

I could not bear a second meal in the mess hall with the Red Guards jeering at me all the time. Near the old Great Wall, I found a cheap restaurant that served noodles. The first time I went there I looked at the menu pasted on the wall:

shredded meat with noodles .... 23 fen

salt vegetable with noodles .... 13 fen

plain noodles...................... 8 fen

My mouth watered at the first item. Too expensive. The second item wasn't too bad and cheaper. On second thoughts, I realised I couldn't even afford that, so I settled for a bowl of plain noodles for 8 fen.

Having graduated from Tung Chi University in 1967, my son was sent to Anhui Province, Fengyang County, the poorest county. The policy was that one had to participate in manual labour for one year before being assigned a job. But they forgot all about him and he remained there as a worker in a printing factory for almost ten years. He was a model worker, but what a waste of the college education he had received!

Didi had finished high school in 1961 as a top student but when he took the college entrance exams he was not accepted. He had a capitalist family background and his father had been arrested and was considered a counter-revolutionary. He was determined to try again the following year. In the meantime he did manual labour in the lane, even pulling human manure carts, and he kept up with his self-study.

In 1962, another policy came down. Scholastic standing and not family background were the requirements for entrance to college. This time Didi passed. Of course the Cultural Revolution affected his studies, as students also had to follow the various movements. He took part in the movement to travel to Beijing where he managed to contact Lollie; we had heard no news from her since the Cultural Revolution began. At one time before graduation, he was held in isolation in the college and I had to wait until he was finally assigned to work in Anhui Province before seeing him again.

After Didi left for Anhui I started taking trips to visit him and then also to my daughter in Beijing. I would spend six months in Beijing, three in Anhui and three in Shanghai. In Fengyang Didi lived in the dormitory of the Printing Press. This was a row of small rooms with no running water, mud floor, no sanitary conveniences. He was allotted only one small room. Cooking was done in a small room opposite on a stove which used twigs or wood for fuel, using waste paper from the printing press to start the fire. Water was carried from the well quite some distance away.

When my son first went, he said, "Oh there's so much I could bring back to China." He was still very patriotic then, but now he doesn't believe in *this*, he doesn't believe in *that*. He is married with two daughters. He married the daughter of the head of his department in the factory where he worked. One day he wrote to me and said "Mummy, can you afford to send me some fragrant soap?"

I wondered what he wanted that for but I bought two pieces at 37 fen a piece, that's all I could afford, and sent them to him.

Later on he said, "I've met a nice girl."

"Send me a picture," I replied.

So he did, and there she was this girl with a fringe over her eyes. So I wrote back and asked if there was anything wrong with her eyes that she had to hide them under that fringe? But of course, that was just the style.

When I went to visit them I must have appeared quite an

oddity, as many of Fenglin's co-workers came to the room to see me. One of them remarked that I was better dressed than the daughter-in-law. Next time I paid them a visit I wore a dark blue jacket.

My daughter had two children. She was a ballet dancer in Peking, trained by the Russians. She was in Canton doing the "Red Detachment of Women." She was doing a leap on the stage and they had a rug on the floor that was supposed to be nailed down but it wasn't and when she landed she slipped and broke her leg. She fainted right on the stage. She didn't dance anymore, but the company kept her on and now she is everything, interpreter, nurse, etc. ... so she's been all over the world.

THE CULTURAL REVOLUTION

The Cultural Revolution lasted ten years (1966–1976). I cannot recall chronologically what I did, nor how I was treated, but I shall just jot down different incidents as they come to my mind.

First, classes were suspended in the Spare Time College where I was working. We attended political study sessions day in and day out. Our school staff was moved to a building on Yuen Ming Yuen Road. Time and again we attended Big Meetings to accuse some "criminals", either capitalists or intellectuals. Once, the capitalists were told to stand and watch a television showing how a capitalist had returned from Hong Kong. She was the head of a factory and came back with her father's ashes. It showed how well she was treated because she had confessed everything. We had to stand up during the showing of the programme and we leaned against each other or the wall for support.

We were always writing confessions. These were returned after being read and then we were told we hadn't confessed enough and to write some more. I couldn't think or make up any more things to confess, so I started rewriting my daily reports by changing the order of the items and also changing the wording. My articles were written in English and some other member translated them into Chinese. I told them my Chinese wasn't good enough to write in Chinese.

We (the capitalists and teachers with problems) were sent to do manual labour every day. The place where I worked most was at the Arts & Crafts warehouse, and sometimes the Silk warehouse; both were situated beside Soochow Creek. While at these places, we were under the surveillance of the Red Guards who belonged to these corporations, while at home the lane committee controlled us. In the lane, we had to attend meetings every Saturday evening and hand in a written report of what we had done during the week. The Corporation also wanted a report, so I got mine translated by Ella (Pearl's daughter-in-law). She made an extra copy for me to hand in to each place.

Once while doing manual labour at the Arts and Crafts warehouse two other teachers of the Spare Time College were talking with me in English. At the same table were two other workers. One teacher asked me what I was going to do during the lunch break and I told him I was going to the Park Hotel to get some bread. "You know, it's better than before liberation," I said.

When we returned to the warehouse in the afternoon we heard over the loudspeaker that all capitalists were to gather in a room downstairs. We couldn't decide whether we were included and asked the worker supervising us. He said that it probably meant the capitalists of their corporation but there was no harm in our attending. We went down. What a surprise it was to find they were waiting for us! They demanded that those who spoke English should step to the front and I did. Then they insisted that the other two who had spoken English should step forward too. The worker who was sitting at our table while we were waiting turned out to be a Red Guard assigned to watch us.

He came forward and told me to kneel down. I did, and he tapped me on the head. Out of curiosity I looked up to see what he had hit me with. It was a broom. I wondered whether they meant to beat me up, but instead he told me to repeat what I had said while working upstairs and I told them in Chinese. He accused me of lying.

"I understand English," he said, "Didn't you mention the word 'park'? You intended going to the park at lunch time. Who were you going to meet there? and for what?"

I told him I was going to the Park Hotel, not to the park.

"Oh yes," he said, "you claimed that the bread after liberation was no good. Do you deny that you had mentioned the park and bread?"

That shows how things could be twisted. After a few more taps on the head with the broom the meeting was adjourned. He felt he had exposed how bad and dishonest a capitalist was.

During the daytime when I was at home, I was controlled by the Red Guards in our lane. Going out one day they stopped me to ask where I was going. To buy some food I told them. Well, you have to hand in a written statement every time you leave the lane. I went back and made out about ten slips, just mentioning things I might want, such as hot water, vegetables, eggs etc. I put the slips in my pocket and when I was stopped I pulled out one of them and gave it to the Red Guard on duty.

Another rule of the lane was to stand before the Chairman's portrait for fifteen minutes before leaving the lane for work every morning. I did not have a watch so couldn't tell how long I was to stand there. Then I had an idea. I took my alarm clock along with me. One day a Red Guard said, "Time's up, what are you standing there for?"

I looked at my clock, showed it to him and answered: "You are wrong there are still three minutes left."

I was never seriously beaten up during the movement, but my poor sister Pearlie was. The Red Guards who controlled her lane treated her very cruelly. One day I found her sitting in the dark in her bedroom, her face and arms black and blue. Another time when I went to see her, I got as far as the door when the Red Guards stopped me and wanted to know what I wanted. They told me to open the door. I pretended that I did not have the key. They grabbed hold of me and took me to the back entrance of the house next door. They spat in my face and gave me a shove. It wasn't a very hard one but I pretended to fall down. I lay on my back on the wet ground.

"Get up," they shouted.

In a weak voice I replied: "I can't, I have high blood pressure and I'm afraid I can't move. I may have an attack."

That scared them and they pulled me up and told me to go home. In the meantime, Pearl had witnessed the whole scene from the drying-stage on the third floor. She wanted to throw her keys down for me. I hoped she would not, but that would not have stopped them from entering. She had once told me how they came through the windows or over the roof whenever they felt like it.

Next came the movement where the Red Guards and others started travelling all over the country, especially to Beijing to see Chairman Mao. It was all free of charge and many took the opportunity to take a free trip to see other parts of the country as well. The railway stations were in chaos and passengers forced their way into the trains, even through the windows. They were squeezed like sardines.

One day a group of us who remained in Shanghai were called to a meeting. We were given a "Political Task" as they called it. We were to sell watermelons and were assigned to the different fruit shops around town. I was sent to a fruit stall near the Fu Shing Park. We were supposed to sell watermelons but that year the crop was very small so we sold whatever fruit there was. At that time, it was mostly peaches of different varieties. Customers often asked which were the sweetest, but I couldn't tell. One day as the shop was closing I bought one of each kind and tried them out. When fruit shops closed for the day, fruit was much cheaper so I was able to buy them. The next day I was able to recommend which were the sweeter peaches, and the customers were pleased with the service I gave them.

The watermelon season had not arrived, yet every morning a very long queue would be waiting for them. They just would not believe us when we told them we had no news about the melons coming to Shanghai. They were so anxious to get melons that some even went to the waterfront to see if the boats had come in. We started selling salt eggs and frozen suckers instead.

One day a customer asked me to pick three or four good eggs for him, ones with lots of oil. I couldn't tell one from the other so just took a chance and picked a few for him. After he had left, I asked the original owner of the stall to show me how to tell which eggs would be good and oily. He told me that no one knows until they break the egg open and taste it.

Then how was I to pick them for the customers, I asked.

"Just pick up one, turn it around in your hand and point to any spot you happen to see and tell him this egg must be good. You may or may not be correct, but that's the best you can do."

I followed his instructions and the customers never complained, so I guess they were satisfied.

I had worked only a few weeks at the fruit store when again we were summoned back to the office. We were told that all the capitalists in foreign trade were to be sent to Chung Ming Island to work on the farms there. This was to remodel ourselves through manual labour. One of my colleagues called it a "concentration camp". We were given three days to pack and were told to take enough clothes for all four seasons. We had no idea how long we were to be there.

Chung Ming Island is at the mouth of the Whampoa River. I was assigned to the East Wind farm. The China National Transportation Corporation capitalists were also stationed there.

There were no other female members in the group, so a teacher from the Workers Trade School was sent to watch over me. We were put in the same quarters as the female cadres from the Transportation Corp. who were to supervise the capitalists.

Cleaning the wooden commode was one of my daily tasks. A cadre was supposed to work with me each day. There were seven of them, so a different one helped me carry the commode to the edge of the pit every day; that is as far as they would go. After that I had to empty the commode into the pit, carry it to the stream and wash it, and then carry it back to the dorm. This commode was big with no handles so you can imagine what difficulty I had carrying it alone. Once some youngsters working on the farm criticised the cadres by saying it wasn't right for them to make me work alone, but that was the cadres' idea of how I should be treated in order to re-mould myself. The youngsters said "We think they need re-moulding themselves." I could make no comments.

At the farm I did anything and everything I was told to do. Once they asked for volunteers to go to widen the river bed. I decided to go too. Actually I was always curious to learn and see new things. Since I did not have the strength to dig up the mud, I was asked to take care of the makeshift stove and boil water for the workers. The fire was already lit when I took over and I just had to add twigs or straw to keep it going. Suddenly I noticed the fire was going out.

I put my head inside the stove to see what was wrong. A gust of wind came down the chimney and the twigs burst into flames. My face was covered with soot, while part of my hair and eyebrows were burned off. I must have looked a sight. When I got back to the farm I was rewarded with an extra thermos of hot water. We were only allowed one thermos a day and this was for drinking as well as washing. An extra thermos of hot water was a real luxury.

It was also one of my duties to fill the thermos every morning. The cadres expected me to fill theirs as well. One day I slipped and broke one of their bottles. I had to buy two thermos vacuums for the bottles as that is what they expected me to do. That was a big part of the six yuan I had to live on each month.

We also had to turn the hay and sun it. I picked a load of hay and turned it over. There lay twelve tiny white mice. I was scared out of my wits.

"Step on them, kill them!" they shouted."

I just couldn't do it, I wasn't accustomed to rats yet.

Besides doing eight hours manual labour every day, we had to attend political studies and write articles. There wasn't much time to rest or sleep. After a few months, it was decided to send me to another part of the farm. This was where the capitalists from the National Machinery Corporation were. I belonged to that Corporation. The reason was that I was the only female member from foreign trade at this place and the teacher who was supervising me was going to be transferred to a May 7 cadre school. As usual, I had to follow orders but I was getting used to life at this farm as I found all the capitalists there were friendly and easy to get along with. I did not cherish the idea of moving.

Life at this part of the farm was much stricter and harder than the one I had left. The capitalists there were different too. I found they were forever reporting to the supervising cadres the failings or faults of others. I realised they were doing this in order to give the cadres a better impression of themselves. I found it rather petty.

I will give here a few examples of the work we did and the way we were treated. The female members were once assigned to work as helpers to the masons who were putting up some buildings. The masons started work at sunrise (they quit early too). That meant we had to be up at 5:00 a.m. to be on duty, without any breakfast. We were glad when that piece of work was over.

During the Cultural Revolution only certain films were allowed to be shown. It was everyone's duty to see these films. One morning we were pulled out of bed at 3:00 a.m. to attend an outdoor film. We trudged through the muddy fields in the dark to reach the site where the film was to be shown. Then we had to stand there and watch it. It was both difficult to see or hear anything. What an ordeal!

The cadres who supervised us were changed every six weeks. Just as we were getting used to one group the new batch came down. They all had their own ways of treating us. Some considered us criminals and took every opportunity to find fault and criticise anything we did. Once a capitalist put his cold hardboiled egg at the bottom of his bowl to warm it up when it was covered with hot rice. He was accused of being greedy, eating too well, and trying to hide the egg under the rice.

While working in the fields one day I asked another capitalist to do a certain piece of work. A cadre shouted at me not to make idle conversation instead of working. We had to accept this treatment. Perhaps it taught me to be patient and not to answer back.

After many months, we were told there would be an adjustment in our maintenance fees. We were to compare ourselves with the "poor, honest farmers" who lived nearby and decide how much we thought we should receive. From inside information I learned that the lowest sum was 60 yuan while the highest for the very progressive ones would be 100 yuan. We had to write down our qualification and requests. In my article I said that compared to the poor farmers who worked so hard I wasn't worth a cent but I hoped the leaders could consider giving me 50 yuan. I got 60 yuan. I felt rich after having existed on six yuan for such a long period.

One capitalist wrote that he'd like to receive 120 yuan. He was singled out, a meeting was called and he was accused of refusing to re-mould properly; he still had capitalist thoughts which he was supposed to get rid of.

A supervising cadre criticised me severely for writing my articles in English. He called me a "foreign slave", etc., and said that from now on I was to write only in Chinese. I did the best I could, but he was shocked when he saw my first paper as half the words were wrong. I told him I was trying. I did study hard the political articles in Chinese, and actually improved to the point where I could write "Big Character Posters." I could talk and write to criticize others, using quotations from Chairman Mao's works.

A meeting was held to decide which capitalists had progressed most. Some named each other. Then the supervising cadre said, "Haven't you forgotten someone?" SILENCE. Then he said "Has no one noticed how Guo Wan Ying has progressed?"

He told me to go ahead and tell them how hard I had worked to improve my Chinese.

I said, "It was entirely due to this cadre who had criticised and forced me to learn Chinese. This was the best kind of forcing I have ever had. If he hadn't shown the way, I would never have improved."

Not long afterwards, the oldest capitalists on Chung Ming Island were to be retired and most of us had already passed retirement age. I was to receive 70 percent of the 60 yuan salary as my retirement fee. In the city, 36 yuan was hardly enough to live on, but somehow I managed.

We were told to start packing, but before leaving each was to give a talk on how they would live after returning to Shanghai.

I said I would continue to study hard. I would read Chairman Mao's works every day to learn from him. I would read the Chinese papers and do my best to improve and re-mould. (I might mention here that during the ten years of the Cultural Revolution, no one was allowed to speak English.)

My little talk pleased the leaders, but the others weren't so enthusiastic about my being the only one to receive praise from the leaders. So ended my manual labour period at Chung Ming.

I returned to Shanghai and started a life of retirement. In the beginning it was not much fun, as 36 yuan a month was hardly enough to live on. The small room I lived in was frightfully cold in winter, and suffocatingly hot in summer. There was only a small window facing north and there was no breeze at night. I used to sit on a stool in the stairway in order to catch a draft from the neighbour's room which faced south. I graduated from a coal ball stove to a kerosene stove so I did my cooking in the bedroom. That made cooking easier.

I had to attend manual labour in the lane a few times each week. We were building air-raid shelters. I had to attend political study groups at the Machinery Corporation, the unit I was retired from. Later we were told to join the political study groups in the lane. However, the educational level of these people was not very high, so I did not have to work too hard to join in discussions at these meetings.

New policies were forever being made. After the Cultural Revolution ended, we were informed that the government would give us back all our back salaries. We had to make out a list. I'm no good at figures, so I had to get David (whom I had married in 1976) to work out the list for me. I was given back all sorts of amounts besides the salaries. I was given the equivalent of US$8,000 which Willie had returned to me during the Cultural

Revolution. I was surprised, as I understood it had gone to pay part of Y.H.'s fine. I felt fabulously rich and I had to start paying my debts, such as ten years' rent which I could not pay while living on a six yuan a month maintenance fee.

RETURNED GOODS

I often received notices telling me to go to certain places to receive some of the goods which were confiscated during the Cultural Revolution. The first time I was instructed to go to a church where confiscated goods were stored. Some of my colleagues were sure I was going to get a lot of things, so they borrowed a mini-bus for me. All I got was a white jade thumb ring. It was already cracked and I don't remember ever having seen it before.

Another time when I received a notice I went and received a package of costume jewellery but most of it wasn't mine. Then I was notified to go to the Machine Corporation to receive some things. Confiscated goods were laid out everywhere, on the tables and on the floor, and we were told to identify our own belongings. The only thing I recognised was a safe box in which I kept Percy's collection of Chinese stamps. I identified the box but they told me the combination lock had been changed. They opened it up and poured out the contents. It was a set of *mah jong*, tiles. I gazed in amazement. "Where are the stamps that were in it?" I asked. "This is what we received from the Foreign Trade Bureau Red Guards," they replied.

The searching of my home took place while I was working at the Spare Time College for Foreign Trade. I was loaned to that school by the China National Machinery Corporation, so the Red Guards of the Foreign Trade Bureau had searched my house.

Then they asked me if the *mah-jong* set was mine. I said that it seemed so, so they asked how many tiles are there in a set? I didn't know. I played a lot of *mah-jong* in the old days but I had never countered the number of tiles. "Then this set is not yours," they said and did not give it to me.

I noticed piles of photos and snapshots strewn around. Unfortunately, mine were all destroyed by the teachers of the Spare Time College. Since classes were suspended the teachers had nothing to do, so they spent time tearing up my pictures, more than thirty albums full. I also lost a whole shelf of my cookbooks and my sewing notes as well as other notes I had kept. I had also kept a memory book for Didi which included all his school reports starting from kindergarten till he was in college. They destroyed that too, something Didi could not forgive. I was even criticised for keeping in his memory book four of his baby teeth that the dentist had extracted at one sitting.

Another time, I was sent to a storehouse to collect a silver hand mirror which was part of my dressing table set. I told them there were more than ten pieces in the set. They informed me this was all they had come across and they would return the other pieces if they ever came across them.

Another time we were taken by bus to Tai Zang, a suburb of Shanghai, to identify goods. There were hundreds of Chinese paintings hung high up. It made me dizzy to look at them. They had taken over 100 of my paintings, but I could not recognise them among this lot. People were supposed to put their name on the paintings they thought were theirs. I noticed that some of the good paintings had over ten names pinned to them. It would be decided later who was the real owner.

Then there was the book section. I roamed around the shelves and decided I would claim a bible and a cookbook. I got them as no one else had put in a claim. There were just shelves and shelves of such books. I wondered what system they used to return things since so many of the items given to me were not mine. And when would this returning of confiscated goods come to an end? Such a waste of time and energy.

Just before I left for the United States in December 1987, my piano was returned, of course in very bad condition. It was one of the policies that capitalists were to get back their pianos. First they had to trace where they were. Once they took me to Fengyi, a suburb of Shanghai, to identify my old piano. When I got there I only found broken boards, strings and keys strewn all around. There was only one whole piano left but I was told someone else had claimed it.

Then I was told that my piano was in Soochow. We started off on another wild goose chase. It was a cold windy day and I was soaked to the skin. We arrived at the home of the person who was supposed to have the piano. It wasn't mine. The piano they took from me was a "Moutrie". We had it in all three houses we had lived in, and I took it with me when I moved to Wuyi Road as Mum was staying with me then. Next I was told the piano was probably in Changsha. Then later they traced it to Guangzhou (Canton). They asked if I cared to go and identify it, but I refused; Guangzhou was too far away. I could hardly believe it when I was told the piano had been identified and brought back to Shanghai. It was the responsibility of the corporation to have it repaired. A very bad job was done. Lollie said she'd like to have it, so it is sitting in Yat Sun's house waiting to be shipped to Beijing. Lollie's new apartment hardly had room for it but she wanted it for sentimental reasons as both she and Deedums took music lessons on that piano. She claimed she had means to repair it in Beijing.

Another policy regarding capitalists came down. Special members (cadres) were chosen to handle this policy in the different foreign trade corporations. I didn't know what to expect. When my turn came, the first question asked of me was what requirements I had. I told him I'd like to get it made clear what my status was.

"But you signed a paper stating you were a capitalist," I was told.

"I did that because I was forced to," I replied.

I then explained that at that time I was a member of a capitalist family but that did not mean I was a capitalist. I had no shares in my husband's private firm, my work was that of an employee and I had no authority in the company.

They told me to find someone in our original private firm to certify to this. Luckily, I found someone to do this, so I was no longer considered a capitalist. I was presented with a framed certificate saying I was gloriously retired. At that time, capitalists did not receive such certificates. I then asked what about my being searched by the Red Guards and all the things they had confiscated. I was told nothing could be done. They were sorry that a mistake had been made.

My next request was to find out how long I was to continue paying Y.H.'s fine? I was told to go to the court and find out. I did and learned that his case had been closed some time ago and I was no longer required to pay any more. I reported this to the cadre in charge and it so happened that a member of the Machinery Corporation was present. I pointed at him.

"Why, just the other day you asked me when was I going to pay up," I said.

"I wasn't talking to you, but to someone else," he replied.

But no one else had been there. What a LIE. Anyway, I had gotten back the equivalent of US$38,000 that Wally had remitted during the Cultural Revolution. I had been forced to write letters demanding money, and Wally was the only one who had responded.

I have been asked why I didn't leave after 1949. The reason is that my children were here and my husband and I had started an international consulting firm in Shanghai. We were just beginning to make money on the scientific instruments and were doing very well, and we didn't have anything outside of China. Where would we go? The rest of the family had gone to New York, Hawaii, Hong Kong, and other locations and I was not going to ask my brothers to support me. And I did not know if the officials would have let me go.

Later, when my younger brother left, my daughter and I went to the railway station to see them off. My daughter was very progressive at the time and turned to me and said, "Such good material leaving. What a big mistake they're making."

My brothers were always very generous with me, but I don't know if my sisters-in-law would have liked having me around. People also asked me why I didn't go to America. But I don't admire the life they live there. When I later went to the United States to visit, I didn't like it as there was no family life, at least not the family life I'm used to.

People are brought up differently there. In China when I had a home and children, we had dinner together and no one left the table until everyone was finished. When I was in America, I cooked a meal for my son's family because I had nothing to do. I put the food on the table and my grandson grabbed a bowl and a plate and piled on the food. I asked where he was going and he said to watch TV.

I also stayed because I wanted to see what was going to happen. People ask me if I regret staying in China. But I never have regrets. People say: "Oh, you have had such a hard life." But there were many more who led lives even harder than mine.

THE END

THE MODERN SHANGHAI, I don't know what it's all about. All these strange people on the streets, and the way they dress and the way they behave. I'm not used to it. I'm old-fashioned. I don't go to these nightclubs, karaoke, or whatever they're called. I haven't even asked what karaoke is. I went once and once only to a disco and got dizzy looking at the lights, and yet they all seemed to be enjoying it. That wasn't my idea of nightlife like in the old days.

I have no contact with the current Kwoks. Someone said the Kwoks are here, do you want to meet them? I said what do you mean? I'm two generations above them, so if they want to meet me, they may come and look me up. I knew their grandparents. So I don't go looking up the younger generation. They don't even know I exist.

I read an article about the Wing On group that said there are no Kwoks left in Shanghai.

"Well," I said with a laugh, "They haven't killed me yet".

POSTSCRIPT

By Tess Johnston

I FIRST CAME to China on a (long sought) Foreign Service assignment in 1981 to the newly-opened American Consulate General in Shanghai. It was then one of our four new Consulates General in China, in addition to the American Embassy in Beijing.

Incidentally we all – then only seven Americans – felt we were in the best post of all, far from Beijing's (and Shenyang's) winter cold and brown-coal polluted air, the remoteness of Chengdu, and the sweltering heat and humidity that plagued our southern colleagues in Guangdong (formerly Canton).

Shanghai was then, and remains today, the most sophisticated city in China. Until 1949 it had been an international city, the greater part of which had been under the control and influence of the British, Americans, in their International Settlement, and the French in their separate French Concession – with some thirty other foreign nationalities also living all over the city. The Chinese lived everywhere in the city, with the original residents primarily in Old Town, which they called *Chung Hoang Miao* (for the City God Temple located there). With its growth, handsome Western architecture prevailed in the city's business district along the riverfront "Bund" and in the leafy Western suburbs. There was a mélange of languages – especially with the influx of White Russians after the Soviets' 1917 Revolution. English was, however, the language of the city's international business world.

In the early 1980s, the foreign population of Shanghai was still small so the consular staffs entertained each other (except for the Russians and Poles, then nations apart) with parties – the most popular of which ultimately became the Australian ConGen's Friday night "Happy Hour" (which lasted far, far longer). We all also circulated among the varied nations' offerings, their parties, film showings, marathon bridge games, outings, or whatever was on offer.

In those early days housing for diplomats, especially villas for the Consuls General, was still scarce so the Belgian CG's living quarters were in a hotel, formerly the Haig Court Apartments on a boulevard at the outer edge of the former French Concession. This stately old building in a pseudo-Spanish Colonial Revival style was best known to most of us foreigners for containing one of the best restaurants in town (with few competitors in those early days). On the upper floors, however, there remained some of the spacious and stylish old apartments (still untouched by the renovations that would later demolish or compromise most of their charm).

The Belgian Consul General, a delightful multi-lingual (aren't all Belgians?) bachelor had a wide circle of friends and a reputation for being a generous host and a great and frequent party-giver. At one of his lively parties as I made my way around the room greeting our usual small circle of colleagues I noticed a cluster of guests surrounding a lady seated in one corner. She was a diminutive white-haired lady dressed in a classic black brocade Mandarin jacket – and she was Chinese! With the exception of official affairs, Chinese women – and in this case an older woman – were fairly rare at our informal parties. So who was this "people-magnet" who was attracting attendees in succeeding waves?

I made my way across the room to her corner and sat down near her. When there was a break in the circle of courtiers who surrounded her I introduced myself – and rather cheekily I suppose – asked what it was that all these people wanted to talk to her about? Was she a former diplomat, a retired Chinese official? Or perhaps an actress? Even in her old age she was very attractive with her halo of white hair, her beautiful light complexion – free of any make-up – and bright eyes that sparkled with intelligence.

She laughed and said, no, she was just an old Chinese who happened to speak English. Even after her brief answer I noticed that her English was almost without accent, neither a Chinese nor a posh British one, indicating that she was not Hong Kong bred, but with just a hint of British schooling. This indicated that she was possibly an upper-class Chinese from either Shanghai or abroad. It took me a bit of mild interrogation to find out that she was both.

She was Daisy Kwok or—now, by Chinese government mandate, no longer in Cantonese but in Pinyin—Guo Wan Ying. Her father had founded the famous Wing On department store, still there on Nanjing Road but now under a Chinese name and with a branch—the one I knew a bit better—in Hong Kong. The Shanghai store was one of the "Big Four" department stores founded by Australian (or "Overseas") Chinese in the early part of the 20th Century. These four massive and once-ornate stores were still there, now under new Chinese names and management, with all-Chinese merchandise and still doing a brisk local business.

We chatted on, midst momentary breaks as she acknowledged new intermittent introductions, and I discovered that she lived quite near me in a lane in the former French Concession. Both our residences lay near Huaihai Lu (the former Avenue Joffre, the main thoroughfare) and in old buildings – mine in an old apartment building, hers in an old villa. Although Chinese, she was actually a foreigner, confirmed much later when she was reissued her Australian passport in a ceremony in the Australian Consulate General in Shanghai. We had already established a rapport based on my interest in learning about the lives of the foreigners in old Shanghai and I had gotten a few enticing glimpses of her life as an upper-class Chinese.

Daisy invited me to come by for tea the next weekend and gave me her address with detailed instructions on how to find her small lane only a few long blocks west of me. The party began to wind down (although there were hints that a private, guys-only party would probably follow). As her host had arranged for Daisy a ride back to her home, we bade each other farewell in anticipation of meeting again soon.

The following Saturday, I strolled up Huaihai Lu and turned right into Hunan Lu, a smaller street. The lovely tree-lined and sometimes over-arched street in this residential area was still lined with its original villas and small apartment houses, some in the 1930s Art Deco style. Now, however, all were shabby and showed clear signs of over-occupancy. The apartment houses were in bad repair, their staircases crammed with boxes, old furniture and other detritus (often covered in layers of dust) that would not fit into flats. Where formerly one family had lived, now each room housed a different tenant with all sharing the kitchen and bath.

That was also the pattern in the villas. Their once neatly-tended gardens were now wastelands crisscrossed by clotheslines and encroached upon by sheds and makeshift additions; their old windowless garages each now housed a whole family. The housing shortage in central Shanghai in the early 1980s had become acute when those who had been sent to the countryside during the so-called "Cultural Revolution" of 1966-76 had now returned to their home city and the government-assigned housing was further stretched to its limits.

Daisy was one of those returnees. Her address proved to be a small villa in much the same condition as the ones I had been accustomed to seeing in Shanghai: a once attractive residence now the victim of benign neglect. A cracked sidewalk led up to a rather nice Art Deco style doorway – but it was downhill from there on. The dark entrance hallway led to rooms with mostly closed doors to my left while a battered oaken staircase on the right led to the second floor where Daisy's current home lay.

All the doors on both sides of the upper hallway were open, so I looked into the first room on the right where several old people were sitting – but none of them was Daisy. When I asked for Guo Wan Ying, one of them motioned to my right so I moved on to the second door just beyond, where I saw Daisy walking toward me with a welcoming smile as she gestured to me through her open door.

I had been in a few homes of my older Chinese friends (referred by their children in the United States) so I knew what to expect. Daisy's room was neat and clean but it seemed small because it was filled with furniture lining all the walls. These were even further diminished by three doors, one leading to the room of other elderly tenants whose larger room adjoined Daisy's, one to the shared bathroom, and one to the hallway from which we had entered. Everything was worn and shabby and I could only contrast in my mind how different it had once been and how very far she had descended from her former gilded life.

Daisy had come to Shanghai from Australia as a young girl, so she had seen the city grow and prosper – and certainly the family's Wing On Department Store. In 1934, she had married Y.H. Woo and raised their daughter (born in 1938) and son (born in 1943) in increasingly difficult circumstances.

Y.H. had turned out to be a hopeless businessman who failed

at almost all his business endeavors and, sadly, was a playboy and – like typical upper-class Chinese men of that era – an unfaithful husband. He also lived mostly off Daisy's money but, when asked why she had chosen Y.H. over her numerous and very wealthy suitors, Daisy replied that it was because he never bored her. Surely there was more to it than that, but we will never know.

Although Daisy's many photograph albums were long ago destroyed by the Red Guards, she had fortunately been able to retrieve duplicates of many of the photographs and some were there in her humble room. This included her stunning bridal photo of 1934. It was Y.H.'s family who had managed to somehow save the photos and get them out of China to Singapore, where Daisy had later gotten them from her in-laws.

Daisy had also married a second time in 1975 to David Wang, an Oxford graduate whom she had met in one of the labor camps, but he died of cancer two years later; there was small photo of him in her flat. The photos of Daisy herself were in the stylish Chinese dress known as a *qipao* before 1949 (and to most foreigners as a *chongsam,* from the Cantonese word). But starting in 1953, she was always in simple Chinese clothing. I did, however, manage to take a photograph of her much later in front of the family's old villa on Lucerne Road at the same spot as her engagement photo with Y.H. Woo many decades earlier; this time, however, alone and in a simple black *qipao.* Over her protests and to make it look a little less severe, I looped strands of my own pearls around her neck.

Several framed items on the walls were certificates. The one that Daisy pointed out to me with great pride was an "Honorable Retirement" certificate. It was awarded her for the labor, including the English teaching, she had been assigned to do as part of her many labor assignments; all this had been finally acknowledged in the certificate awarded her a decade later, the one of which she was the proudest. She had actually enjoyed her teaching and had even designed a curriculum that was more effective than the standard one she was handed (thus earning her the enmity of her male colleagues). Directed on to other jobs utilizing her English fluency she had, as always, tried to do her best in everything she did, hence her great pride in this acknowledgement of her service and her skills.

The modest furniture in the room consisted of a double bed, a square *mah-jong* table with several straight-backed wooden chairs, a small cabinet, a bookcase overflowing with books, and a tall, old-fashioned wooden wardrobe that took up most of the remaining space. All of this old furniture was of course shabby but the overall effect, perhaps reflecting the occupant, was not depressing but rather reminded one of old photos of a typical *tingzejian*, the rooms of poor scholars usually located on the north side of a *shikumen* rowhouse and above the kitchen.

This corner room was, however, in an old villa and was a bright one with high ceilings and two of its walls pierced by long windows that let in sunlight and fresh air (and cold air in the winter). Daisy invited me to have a seat at the table while she prepared the tea. This table was for dining and served also as the "study" table she used when teaching English to the young Chinese students who increasingly sought her out to tutor them. There were many, so many in fact that she now limited her lessons to the children of friends or to ones recommended by those friends.

From a cabinet she produced cups and saucers, some slightly chipped, and a sugar bowl and creamer. There were also cookies from a round tin that I recognized as a well-known Chinese brand. Daisy set the table and poured the tea in a skilled and gracious manner that indicated she had once been quite familiar with the niceties of serving an afternoon English tea. Somehow it was easy to imagine her doing that in another setting, long long ago and in a different room – and era. I thought of it as being in another life, as it seemed impossible that one's life could change so dramatically in four decades – not from the proverbial "rags to riches" but obviously more from the riches downward.

As I summed up in the chapter on Daisy in my book *Frenchtown Shanghai*, "…unbowed by decades of turmoil that robbed her of almost everything she owned and loved, she showed no resentment. In her last twenty-five years Daisy accepted her reduced circumstances with equanimity. She was increasingly the center of a large circle of friends, students, journalists and admirers from around the world. Although the silverware no longer matched and the cups were chipped she still poured tea for her guests as graciously and elegantly as if she were in the drawing room of her youth."

One of the family's servants, the only one from that earlier life, was still in her life. He was Song Lin, who had started working for the family at a very early age, had gone back to his family in the countryside in the 1950s, but had returned to Shanghai in time to take care of Daisy when she finally made her last move to Hunan Lu. He lived far away in a northern suburb of the city but as she got older he visited her often, where I first met him. He brought her prepared food or often various foodstuffs that he prepared for her after he got there. Although they maintained a hint of the old master and servant formula, he had now become her loyal friend and companion on whom she heavily relied.

He was a sturdy-looking peasant with a calm and confident disposition and he obviously adored Daisy and was determined to help her in any way he could. As she became increasingly old and more frail he was at her home more often. (Ultimately he assumed responsibility when she died, as her children were far away and it took some time for them to get to Shanghai to take over.)

My conversations with Daisy were wide-ranging but many of them were in response to my queries about her past life. I knew she had stayed in China after 1949 but I did not know the details of why, nor of how she had managed to survive the turbulent years that followed. Her own words are in this book so I will not dwell on them here, but over our many meetings in her remaining years I got these stories in more vivid detail than any written narrative can convey.

I will therefore confine my own narrative here to two stories of our weekend, usually bi-weekly, meetings – when I had free time. I loved her company, but as I had a busy work life at the Consulate-General and a circle of friends and colleagues whom I often saw after work, I had decided to devote some of my weekends to taking her in my car to various places she had spoken about but had not seen in many years. She started calling these her little "Adventures." Some were in the city and others in the nearby countryside. These two represent typical places to which we made our weekend drives.

I started our trips by taking her to the country villa of Sir Victor Sassoon, the famous Sephardi Jewish tycoon who owned – and lived in – the Cathay Hotel on the Bund, but often entertained at his home in the western suburbs. Daisy knew him and had been to some parties out at his Tudorbethan villa in a vast expanse of gardens on Hongqiao Road. At that time it was still accessible to the few who knew a back way in through the gardens. I was one.

We parked in a nearby hotel parking lot and strolled down the path with no problem in approaching the villa. We circled it, past the servants' quarters and a small stable with a well at the back of the house and emerged under the long grape arbor on its west side. When we reached the front veranda again, we peered through the long windows facing the verdant front garden and lawn nearest to the highway.

There was the long, wood-beamed great hall with a fireplace (big enough to roast an ox) and a minstrels' gallery, the small wooden balcony at one end with a Tudor rose, a Scottish thistle and an Irish clover carved and painted on it. We spent a lovely afternoon there sitting on the terrace in a double lawn swing that had been left outdoors, perhaps when the villa had been used for some special events.

I always tried to vary our Adventures, sometimes in town and sometime into the countryside around Shanghai, like a trip down to the south coast nearest Shanghai called Jin Shan Wei. There we picnic'd atop a massive old concrete gun emplacement (Japanese or Nationalist? – we did not know) while looking out at the muddy waters. On the foreshore, the locals with pails and spades dug for small edible sea creatures that we could not see.

But we did see – and I can hardly believe it even today as I have never seen it anywhere else – fish crawling out of holes, skittering across the mud, and then diving into yet other holes. We named this mind-boggling phenomenon and its location "The Bay of the Walking Fish".

Many of our trips were just ones within the city and more routine, but Daisy always seemed to thoroughly enjoy them. She seldom went far from her neighborhood, where she could walk to the markets but she sometimes took local buses to places a little farther afield to find things not found in local shops. In the 1980s, few Chinese, except for officials, had access to automobiles so you can imagine what a treat it must have been for her – as for me – to be able to get out of town and, for her, even to "downtown" with such ease.

I felt so fortunate to be able to enjoy her company on a fairly regular basis and I tried to remember and take her to places that she had mentioned from her early years in Shanghai. Certainly the Bund, Nanking Road, including the family's Wing On Department Store – and its three Overseas Chinese "rival" stores, the Sincere, the Sun, and the Sun-Sun – and then on to the Park Hotel, still functioning in a sadly diminished version, where she had once started a small fashion business with her Chinese friend.

Over the years, when we did our drives we must have gone by, or to, some of the places where Daisy had suffered so much deprivation and humiliation during the post-1949 years. She sometimes would mention it, as when we drove by the old Ward Road Jail (the "D-Lay-Jao", now Tilanqiao, of her narrative) but it was never with rancor, regret, bitterness, or any indication of the hard times she had gone through. For her the past was past, and the future always held promise, as she was interested in so many things, both old and new. I often wondered if I could ever have maintained that attitude in the face of so much suffering and gross injustice. I feel sure I could not.

I was of course not always there for Daisy, what with my own travels (and my semi-annual "Home Leaves") but she never lacked companionship and callers. Many of my friends wanted to meet her, but I self-selected only the more interesting ones, and tried to make it at a tea in my home or during an Adventure as I did not want to overburden her.

Daisy always had newsmen and correspondents, both TV and newspaper ones, wanting to interview her and over the years I have heard some of the resulting tape recordings. My favorite one is from the BBC's Clive James where he asked Daisy how many servants she had.

"Twenty-four," she replied. "That's all."

I cannot report on Daisy's last days, as her death came as a total surprise to me. I had, sadly, waited too late and did not get to see her in her last week as I simply did not realize that she was that near the end. When I got the call that she had died, on September 25, 1998, a week after my birthday, I was totally unprepared for it and was devastated.

I knew I was expected to go to the funeral or memorial service – but I just could not; I could not bear the idea of saying my goodbye to her in that public forum. As a notorious "weeper," I knew that I would cry my heart out at this final tribute to her. So I took the coward's way out, and used the "loophole" that is the custom in China, that anyone over the age of fifty – and I was then 67 – is not required to attend funerals. I sent flowers.

Thus I will always remember Daisy, still vivid in my mind's eye, as she once was, alive and vital – and interested in everything. But, alas, I did not get that Last Goodbye.

About The Author

Daisy Kwok was born in Australia in 1908 and moved with her family to Shanghai in 1918. Her father founded the largest department store in East Asia, the Wing On Department Store and Daisy for decades lived the life of the rich and famous and one of the world's most dazzling cities. Then came the Japanese invasion in 1937 and the communist takeover in 1949, and unlike so many other wealthy residents, Daisy decided to stay in Shanghai, and was denounced as a capitalist before being rehabilitated in the late 1970s. She died in Shanghai in 1998.

www.ingramcontent.com/pod-product-compliance
Lightning Source LLC
Chambersburg PA
CBHW011239120626
46549CB00009B/3332